7-25-79

To Herb,

After fourscore years
and ten, the best
years are still ahead

Love,
Alice

I0575620

CHINA

The ideograph above is the Chinese for "the dream of man."
It was brush written by Tien Lung.

CHINA:

The Dream of Man?

by Tore Zetterholm

with photographs and captions by
Bo Gärtze

edited by Ray Freiman

RIDGEWAY
EDITIONS

Text copyright © 1977 by Tore Zetterholm
Photographs copyright © 1977 by Bo Gärtze

All rights reserved.

No part of the contents of this book may be reproduced
without the written permission of the publishers,
RIDGEWAY EDITIONS
16 Ridgeway Plaza,
Stamford, Connecticut 06905
to whom all requests for information should be addressed.

Published simultaneously in Sweden by
Bokförlaget Bra Böcker, Höganäs.

Library of Congress Catalog Card No.: 77-84470
ISBN 0-89589-000-3

Design: Folke Müller and Hans Enblom
Printed and bound in Austria

TABLE OF CONTENTS

PAGE

The Four Cornerstones of Modern China

FOOD   6

CHILDREN   15

INDUSTRY   25

IDEOLOGY   32

TRAVEL IN TIME & SPACE   37

THE EMPERORS OF CHINA   44

China's Imperial Dynasties   78

THE REVOLUTION   80

BEFORE AND AFTER   92

Mao Tse-tung   97

A RICH WELL FULL OF WATER   98

TWELVE ON ONE CYCLE   135

350 MILLION WOMEN

BECOME HUMAN BEINGS   144

THE YOUNG AND THE OLD   155

Schools in China   156

Sports in China   172

YOU ARE OUR VOICE   184

THE DREAM OF MAN   212

Map of China   238

FOOD

is the first of the four cornerstones of modern China. Production of its daily bread is one of the fundamentals on which the China of today is building. Over eighty per cent of the population is engaged in agriculture. For the first time in thousands of years, starvation has been eliminated.

China, with its 800 million people, is the largest national population group on earth. To visit the country today is to meet a nation in the midst of a gigantic developing process, to witness a colossal experiment with people and new forms of co-existence.

1962: After three years of bad crops, the produce market in Wuhan (recent population 2,900,000) was a sorry sight. ▼

Ten years of good crops and modernized distribution have changed all that. ▶

▲ *Before the Revolution, the average Chinese could not be sure of even a bowl of steaming rice. In the first decades after 1949, people lived dangerously close to hunger. The Revolution set out to conquer this age-old enemy.*

▲ *Today, huge quantities of food are stored against the possibility of future crop failures.*

Freshwater fishing, with primitive tools and methods, is at best unreliable.

Today large fish farms and modern deep-sea fishing methods guarantee a steady ample yield.

CHILDREN

are the next cornerstone. Modern China treasures its children, its youth, the new generation. Determined concentration on the health and education of the young in the decades since the Revolution of 1949 is apparent everywhere.

◀ *An earthen floor and poor equipment were once quite common in village schools during the nineteen sixties.*

◄ *Traditionally, it was the old people who took care of the infants in the simple farm homes of the countryside.*

On a school excursion to the mountains the children in China are quiet and well-behaved. Fights and rows are rare, thanks to the new teachings which consciously combat the spirit of competition between the children. There are no material rewards in the schools. The communists owe much of this philosophy to the strong old moral tradition of Confucianism. ▼

◄ *A lesson in a well-appointed nursery school in Peking, in the 70s. Here the children are trying to "imitate the teacher."*

17

Yu-Gi and her mother are readying themselves for a Sunday walk. The parents are industrial workers in Shanghai, and they live in an apartment which consists of two rooms and a kitchen. Their rent is just $3.00 a month! This may be one of the reasons why salaries are just a fraction of ours. An average worker earns about $25.00 a month, but in reality such comparisons tell us little.

▲ *Organized training for small boys on a local sports playground in Peking.*

Decorative propaganda at the infants' playground in Canton. ▶

19

Swimming in the big lake in the Lu-Shan mountains is great fun, especially when you have borrowed a floating plastic pillow. The girls are swimming in their dresses, not because of modesty, but because of the shortage of cloth. On my previous trip I saw how carefully they arranged their manufacturing priorities.

▲ *Helping their elders with with the daily chores is a matter of course for the children of China.*

◄ *Young pioneers at play singing a song about work in the rice fields.*

21

What fun! It's a pity that boys are always so suspicious.

INDUSTRY

is the third Chinese cornerstone. Twenty-five years ago no one could imagine that this underdeveloped, war-ravaged country would accomplish so much in technology, science, and industrial production in so short a time.

◄ *Steelworkers in protective asbestos clothing.*

▲ *The great steelworks in Wuhan started their production in 1958 with a capacity of three million tons a year.*

◄ *A basic principle of the new China's industrial development is in Mao Tse-tung's words, "to preserve our own independence, keep the initiative in our own hands, and trust our own strength."*

Modern hydraulic power is used to press steel for axles. ▶

Lubricating a faithful old servant vintage 1951. ▼

▲ *Workshop industry is being developed on a very large scale. Here in Shanghai a worker is turning out precision machinery.*

Today Loyang leads in production of caterpillar tractors "Made in China."

◀ *A modern cotton-spinning mill in Peking, with 3,000 fully automatic looms under one roof.*

▲ *Students making adjustments in equipment, at the oil fields in Taching, Heilungkiang province.*

31

IDEOLOGY

is the fourth of the cornerstones. Education and social reform are not aimed exclusively at raising the people's living standards, but are also intended to create "the new socialist man." The cornerstone of that new man's thinking is the ideology of Chairman Mao.

Intensive development of agriculture is proceeding in the new communes in Tibet. Regdzin Wanggyal is responsible for cultivation of experimental types of winter wheat on the Lhasa tableland.

Welcoming quotations from Mao greet the visitor at the railway station in Sum-Shun, north of Hong-Kong.

Travel in China is not like travel in Norway or France. Not even the most avid supporter of China would say that. Still, one does have certain illusions when one goes there for the first time—at least I had.

I was used to travel. I didn't think I needed an interpreter or a guide. Why shouldn't I be able to travel on my own? That was how I expressed myself to the Chinese. I was informed, however, that not even the Chinese are allowed to travel freely within their own country. Only a few cities and popular communities have been opened to tourists, but if I insisted on managing on my own in Peking, I was free to try.

I tried for half a day. Then the small traveling-snob within me gave up. I could not contact anybody, nor ask the way, nor order a meal. I was not even able to write the name of my hotel or my street. The characters were an indecipherable muddle of dots and lines. And, should I try to say something, I risked making a mistake. With the four or five different ways of pronouncing the vowels, I might, by mistake, tell someone to go to *hell*.

"Surely there must be someone who speaks English?" asked people at home. That would be just as common as finding someone who speaks Cantonese in the shops and the hotels of Sweden. The day I arrived in Soochou, a city of about one million citizens, they told me that I was the only westerner in the whole city.

In other words, you are totally and helplessly dependent on the interpreter, the guide, and also the travel agency—reduced to the patronizing of hotels and restaurants arranged for use by westerners. Without an interpreter you travel like a deaf mute. This also affects your ability to get information or carry on a casual conversation. *You* are dependent on the interpreter, yet the person to whom you are speaking always has the interpreter as a witness to what *he's* saying.

Almost as indispensable as an interpreter is a bit of knowledge of the background of the Chinese and how their history, social system and living conditions differ from ours. Is it necessary to read about a lot of ancient emperors and wars to understand China today? Yes, it is. Had I only known a bit more, I should have been spared much confusion and irritation during my first visit. Many naive China enthusiasts who believe that the

TRAVEL
IN TIME & PLACE

▲ *With my helpful interpreters Lee and Hu, at the Big Wall on my first trip. Even their knowledge of the language failed, on our zigzag journey through China, from Kwangtung province in the south to Inner Mongolia in the north.*

Chinese Communists have broken with old China's traditions should really learn how much the Red Chinese of today owe to their revolutionary farmer-ancestors and to the old Chinese morality.

Only the most dogmatic can deny that many phenomena in China today are hard to accept for a westerner who is used to comfort and freedom of speech and movement. The most hidebound supporter of our consumption-oriented and competitive society cannot

▲ *Revolutionary farmer-ancestors.*

▲ *In their old religion, the Chinese worshipped ghosts and gods. Here a pious woman is sacrificing to the god of the River, who protects all future mothers.*

escape being filled with enthusiasm over the Chinese people's pleasure in their work, their idealism, their honesty and their concern for the poor and oppressed. One should not make the mistake of thinking that all the harsh measures and all the moral splendor originate from the communist system. Just a little historical knowledge teaches us that the narrow limitations on individualism and private life are no communist invention. We must look for the explanation in the life style and collectivist tradition of old China.

Suspicion and aggression against strangers, especially westerners, are not new. We can find evidence of them in their history of the eighteenth and nineteenth centuries, even though opposition to the capitalist world has become sharper since the revolution. The isolation in international relations for which the Chinese of today are so often blamed is also an old tradition. It can be seen clearly in a famous letter of the eighteenth century in which the Chinese emperor politely, but firmly, declines an English king's proposal for increased trade and diplomatic connections:

As to what you have requested in your message, O King, namely to be allowed to send one of your subjects to reside in the Celestial Empire to look after your country's trade, this does not conform to the Celestial Empire's ceremonial system, and definitely cannot be done ... The Celestial Empire, ruling all within the four seas, does not value rare and precious things ... We have never valued ingenious articles, nor do we have the slightest need of your country's manufactures.

◄ *It is the year of the Cuban crisis, and the steelworkers in Wuhan have gathered for a mass meeting.*

41

▲ *The message of the Cultural Revolution in Shanghai, in 1966. "Farmers, workers, soldiers, are the trinity which will build the country."*

Until recently, Red China was looked upon as a threat to the free world. As proof of China's imperialist ways people point to the annexation of Tibet. The truth is, however, Tibet became Chinese long before Scotland became British. Even something as shocking as the Chinese prohibition of travel within their own country becomes understandable when one considers the chaos during the cultural revolution. At that time millions of young people traveled within the country without restriction, with the result that all communications broke down. Free travel also requires a standard of living which the Chinese have not yet reached. As always in China, *background* is the key word.

Before we can agree or disagree with customs which seem strange and frightening to us, we must investigate their practical explanation or historic background. If we wish to understand the China of today—its harsh foreign policy, its tough domestic discipline, its Cultural Revolution and its dream of the new socialist man—we need to study not only the recent history of China, but also her long, fantastic story. Hers was an empire which started at the time of the oldest Egyptian Pharaohs, and did not end until well into our own century.

In a street in Hangchou. The children very rarely meet a westerner, but some think that it is correct to stick out their tongues at the "foreign devil."

After the teacher explained to them why I was there, I was warmly greeted.

When I visited China for the first time in the middle of the sixties, Pu-Yi, the last emperor, could sometimes be seen in the streets of Peking. By then he had been dethroned, and earned his living as an ordinary government official. He had been allowed to live, despite the fact that he, more than anyone else, was a symbol of the *old* feudal China.

His early life had been like the most exotic oriental fairy tale. He grew up in the Imperial Palace in Peking. It was called the Forbidden City because no ordinary person was allowed to approach it. Even when he was five years old, Pu-Yi was worshipped like a god. Every visitor had to fall on his knees and beat his forehead against the floor nine times. His father and mother addressed him as "Your Majesty"—when he went to play in the garden, a great procession of eunuchs preceded him carrying changes of clothes, unbrellas, parasols, medicines and boxes of tea, cakes and candies on long poles.

The actual ruler of China was the cruel step-mother of the fairy tale, the Dowager Empress Tzu-hsi. She was an intelligent woman but a domineering dictator. Her motto was: "He who gives me a moment of anxiety shall atone for it with punishment all the rest of his life."

Pu-Yi (called Hsüan-tung as emperor) was educated in many useless things, but not in modern history or science. He was cruel to his eunuchs and pages even though he was totally dependent on them. He could not even tie his own shoelaces!

THE EMPERORS OF CHINA

In 1911, when the first revolution came and the republicans dethroned the boy-emperor, he was allowed to continue living in the palace. He retained his title and his enormous allowance—but his world became even more unreal. He was never allowed to appear outside the Forbidden City. Surrounded by intrigue, he lived there until 1924—an exotic animal in a cage. Once he recaptured the throne for a few short weeks, but then had to flee with his wives and concubines, carrying as many art treasures and jewels as they could.

For nearly ten years he sat brooding in Tientsin on the coast, dreaming that the Son of Heaven would one day take revenge on the republicans. His chance came when the Japanese invaded North China and crowned him Emperor of Manchuko. He acted as a puppet ruler for them until the end of the

From a topographical point of view, Peking is a very uninteresting city. The pavilion in the foreground is atop "Coal Hill," which is one of the few high points in the capital. More and more, modern hotels and residences rise over the low traditional buildings.

Second World War and was forced to sign all their measures of terror against the Chinese people. In all of China, no one was hated more than he.

At the end of World War II after the atom bomb and the collapse of Japan, the ex-emperor fled to the Soviet Union. Some years later, he was extradited to China as a war criminal. He was not executed, but instead played a part in one of the most well-produced propaganda campaigns of our century. First, he was put in jail to be brainwashed. Considering his childhood and upbringing, it must have been a trying experience for him to perform any of the practical duties which are required of prisoners.

In 1959 he was pardoned by the People's Republic of China's highest court. In his memoirs, he writes:

"The war criminal Aisin Gioro Pu-Yi of male sex, 54 years old and of Manchurian origin, has now served ten years in prison. He has retrained himself by means of work and ideological education and is now totally transformed. According to Article I in the Law of Special Forgiveness he is now to be set free. . . . My native country has transformed me as a man."

◀ *Schoolchildren from one of Peking's elementary schools, waiting in front of the Tien-An-Men gate for a visit to the old imperial city.*

47

▲ *Here, from the gate of "The Heavenly Peace," the emperor and his court could look out upon the caravans as they approached the city.*

Whether you believe in the honesty of his new conviction or look upon him as a shrewd opportunist, you cannot deny that it was a masterful stroke by the Chinese to have treated his case as a psychological conversion. I myself believe that he was absolutely sincere when describing his conversion from emperor to citizen, but others are more skeptical when they note his eagerness to slander his old imperial self.

Today it is a marvelous experience to see

the Emperor's property and trappings being viewed by Sunday strollers—workers in blue shirts, girl-soldiers with black pigtails and yellow caps, Chinese fathers with their children on their backs and grandmothers with stunted feet in felt slippers. As they walk wide-eyed through the Palace of Complete Harmony and Complete Happiness, they marvel at the imperial wedding-bed and the small diamond-decorated gold pagoda where fallen hair from the cruel dowager-empress's head was kept.

▲ *A system of gates leads to the farthest part of the imperial city, The Forbidden City. These marble steps go up to the Tai-Ho Gate.*

Grotesque lions, cast in bronze and covered with gold, stand at the entrances like mute guardians.

The most astonishing thing of all is that you could have encountered the transformed Emperor on his way to work like any man in the crowd. He died in 1971.

Hsüan-tung, or Pu-Yi, was the last of a line of emperors whose rule stretched back five thousand years. The early outlines of the social system whose traditions still operate in China today—the social system of the river-states—started three thousand years before Christ. In the so-called river-states there were seldom any solitary settlements. From the beginning they were forced to cooperate with, and subordinate themselves to, a central authority which tamed the rivers by building dams and canals. The first of the historically documented imperial families (dynasties) was the Shang, who subdued a number of smaller principalities and formed a "state" in the area of the lower Yellow River valley about 1500 B.C. In an old chronicle it is reported that the emperor taught his people the use of inventions to better their lives. In reality he was not solely responsible for their advanced civilization. It was the ordinary working people who were responsible for cultivating the earth, planting mulberries for the cultivation of the silkworm, and making exquisitely ornamented bronze tools and marvelous ceramics. At this time the hard labor was performed by slaves, whose lives were considered to be worthless. We can read on the bronze tablets that horses were of greater value. When a sovereign died, his slaves were buried with him. From time to time, slaves and the poor rebelled and dethroned the imperial rulers. It has always been this way in China.

Detail from the Nine-Dragon Wall, a powerful protective wall, whose symbols were said to prevent evil spirits from forcing their way into the imperial paradise.

▲ *Tai-Ho-Tien (The Imperial Palace) with its approximately 24,000 square feet, is the largest building in the imperial city. The palace was first erected in 1420, during the reign of the Ming Emperor Yung-Lo.*

▲ *In the Tai-Ho Hall (The Hall of High Harmony) is the famous Dragon Throne.*

Like a huge dragon, the Chinese wall winds across the mountains and valleys of northern China. In spite of all that I had heard and read about it, I was nonetheless awed by its enormous dimensions. It is nearly sixteen and a half feet high, nineteen feet wide, almost one thousand five hundred miles long, and has about twenty thousand watch towers. A prince from the area of Ch'in started building it for defense against the invading Huns. By conquering all the neighboring principalities, he united China into a single state for the first time. From the name of his dynasty, Ch'in, came the words China and Chinese.

Following the Ch'in dynasty came the Han dynasty, which governed with a gentle hand and remained in power for nearly four hundred years. These were China's first days of glory. The Chinese still call themselves the people of Han. The country made rapid progress during those times. Farmers developed better tools, paper was invented, and culture advanced. Yet the powerful Han Dynasty was overthrown by "The Yellow Turbans" during the peasants' revolution at the beginning of the second century B.C.

The next cultural peak was reached during the Tang Dynasty (618–907 A.D.). The country continued to develop and progress was made in many areas. They learned to use coal, (to the great surprise of western travelers

Hsüan-tung, also called Pu-Yi, the last emperor of China, after his transformation into an ordinary citizen.

who had never before seen what they thought to be stones burning). The art of printing with moveable type was invented (in Korea)—several hundred years before Gutenberg. Great canals were built during this time, among them the Imperial Canal which connected the two great water arteries of the country, the Yellow River and the Yang-tze-kiang.

▲ *Today The Forbidden City is a popular museum. Visitors listening to a guide standing in front of a copper urn, coated with gold, which once belonged to the Imperial Fire Fighters.*

◄ *Emperors of the Ming and Ch'ing Dynasties directed all the important ceremonies from the Dragon Throne, surrounded by symbols for a long and happy life (cranes, dragons, etc.) Here the New Year and winter solstice were proclaimed, here the ancestors' ghosts were honored, and here the birthdays of prominent citizens were celebrated.*

▲ *The arrangement of the palaces, with their slender lacquered pillars and beautifully curved roofs, gives the visitor a sensation of space and airiness.*

Chinese goods were exported to the Mediterranean countries by caravan. The caravan routes have been called the "Silk-way" and have been very important to world trade since those times.

It has been said that during the Tang Dynasty every Chinese was a poet. This, of course, included only those who could read—the upper class. Li Po was a poet, life-worshipper and Bohemian. After a time as poet at the imperial court, he resumed a wandering life and is said to have been drowned while drunk, trying to catch the reflection of the moon in a river.

▲ *This kind of sundial has been used in China since before the time of Christ.*

This old woman is sitting in the imperial garden, resting her stunted feet, a relic of times past. ▼

It is impossible to translate Chinese lyric poetry. One might better write a new poem. This is how Erik Blomberg, a modern Swedish poet, interprets Li Po:

"The white heron
falls like a snowflake
against the shore of a dark-blue lake.
On the stone furthest away
it is immobile awaiting
the arrival of the severe winter."

For a long time after the decline of the Tang Dynasty, the country was in chaos. Robbers and corrupt officials cheated the people mercilessly and famine and epidemics raged. A certain degree of order was re-established during the Sung Dynasty. Among other things, the compass and gunpowder were invented as progress and creativity returned to China.

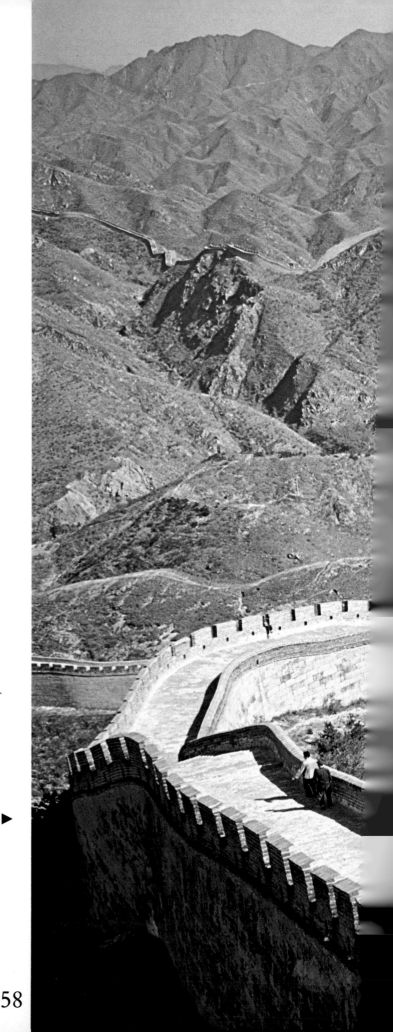

To the north of China live the Mongols, who conquered the greater part of China in less than one century. The first great Mongol chieftain was "the master of the seas," Genghis Khan, whose name became known and dreaded all over the world. The Mongolian rulers of the Yüan Dynasty reigned on China's imperial throne between 1206 and 1370 A.D. Their empire was the greatest that had ever existed up to that time.

The Italian Marco Polo wrote a tale of his journeys to the court of Emperor Kublai Khan in Peking, one of the most remarkable travel books ever written. But in time, as with so many other dynasties, the Mongol rulers were deposed by a peasants' revolution.

When one hears the word Ming one likely thinks of the exquisite blue-white porcelain which bears this name. A Ming vase is a treasure for every collector of antiques. To the Chinese people, the empire of the Ming Dynasty (1368–1644 A.D.) represented a dramatic time. It started when the poor monk Chu Yun-chang, with his peasants' army, expelled the Mongols from the country and declared himself emperor. Succeeding Ming emperors continued to wage war in the north and in the west and thereby established China's present broad frontiers. Although Tibet belonged to China, its control was divided between the Chinese emperor and the Dalai Lama, the spiritual leader of the Tibetans.

In the sixteenth century foreign nations began finding their way to China. In 1516 A.D. the first Portuguese sailed into the port of Canton in southern China. Shortly after that, trade with the Spaniards, the Dutch and the English began. There should have been mutual benefits, but unfortunately the Europeans were too anxious to line their own pockets. Commerce during the following centuries was to China's disadvantage, and consequently it reacted by closing its ports to foreigners.

Like a giant snake, the Great Wall threads its ▶ *way through the countryside. It is 1,500 miles long, as the crow flies, from Kansu province in the west to the Yellow River in the east. To walk the length of the wall, however, one must travel three times that far. Several hundred years before our calendar began, a number of lesser wall systems existed here in the north, as protection from the Mongols. In 200 B.C., the Emperor Shih Huang Ti linked them all together.*

58

▲ *People from Peking often make excursion to this part of the wall.*

◄ *The wall follows the terrain with many steep rises and drops. Staircases were placed at frequent intervals so that soldiers could quickly man the shooting positions.*

There are special patrol towers at strategic points. Millions of slave-laborers built this wall, many of whom never returned home, but were buried inside in the wall. ▶

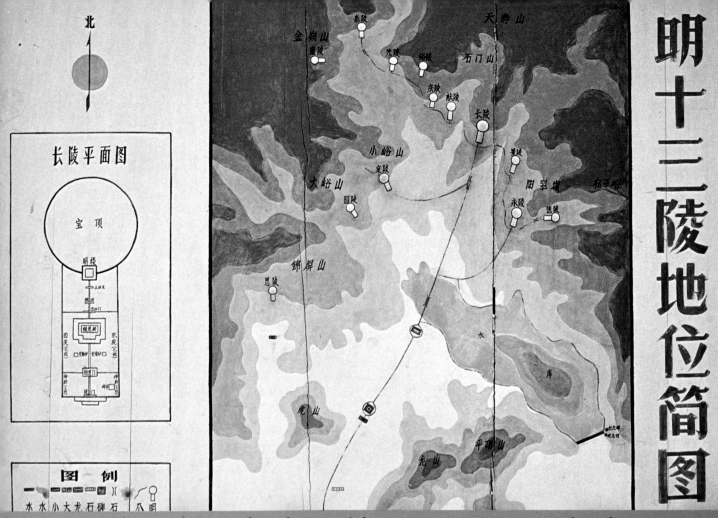

長陵平面圖

北

宝顶

明楼

西庑（宫殿）　稜恩殿　东庑（宫殿）

图例

水水　小大龙石碑石　门明

明十三陵地位简图

▲ *Map showing the area where thirteen of the Ming Dynasty emperors are buried.*

An avenue of silent stone guardian animals and warriors protect the burial grounds against evil spirits and grave-robbers.

▲ *A temple marks the location of the tomb of Emperor Wan-Li.*

Farming was, as it still is, the chief industry. The standard of living of the peasants rose very slowly, and during years of bad harvests, hundreds of thousands starved to death. The Ming Dynasty was overthrown by a farmers' revolution, and Peking was occupied. The last emperor of the dynasty hanged himself from a tree in his own garden.

The next imperial family, the Ch'ing, from Manchuria, came to power after suppressing the rebellious farmers. Ch'ing was the last of the Chinese dynasties. Although it was of foreign origin, it eventually became Chinese in manner and customs even though it forced the Chinese men to wear the well-known long pigtails, which they despised.

The Ch'ing dynasty was even more enlightened than the Ming. It introduced such diverse things as tax exemptions and improved agriculture. During these fruitful years, the population increased greatly. By the beginning of the nineteenth century there were more than 300 million people in China.

Life was still hard for the great masses. They were often forced to go into debt and many had to leave their land and become day-laborers. The sale of children as servants to the wealthy was common, especially in years of famine. Many poor people emigrated. Because of their fear of foreign business competition and attempted coups against their regime, the Ch'ing emperors closed off their country. This isolation delayed industrial development. Agriculture was inadequate, and incapable of supplying the people's needs when harvests failed. Toward the end of the century, the northern provinces were hit year after year by drought and other natural catastrophes. The famine of 1876–79 claimed almost ten million lives. It was the worst tragedy in the history of mankind. When the Manchurian empire declined, the people suffered. Bands of robbers scourged the country, corruption increased, and foreign powers became increasingly ruthless in their penetration and exploitation.

During the Ch'ing Dynasty, the custom of

▲ *The tomb of Emperor Wan-Li (1573–1620 A.D.) was opened in 1956. After a long search, the well-camouflaged route to his sepulchral chamber was found, sixty-five feet below ground.*

▲ *Wan-Li and his two wives were buried side by side in magnificent lacquered coffins.*

65

Following ancient tradition, the Emperor had his burial room prepared and filled with treasures during his lifetime. At the top of the picture you can see Wan-Li's crown, woven of golden thread and rich ornaments. ▼

▲ The imperial household used chopsticks and plates of solid gold. Wan-Li, who is recorded by history as a man who lived most luxuriously, is said to have arranged parties in what was to be his burial room.

The Emperor ordered a marble throne and tabourets to be made for him and his Empresses, so that they could sit in the Kingdom of the Dead as they had in life. ▶

smoking opium became increasingly common in China, and a great part of the population became addicted. The cultivation of opium poppies occupied two-thirds of the arable land in some areas. When the emperor tried to stop the importation of Indian opium, the English declared war to protect their huge profits from the opium trade. China was defeated, and the peace treaty allowed English merchants to sell opium freely. Europeans would also have free admission to a number of Chinese ports, and the biggest cities in China would be open to Christian missionaries. From then on, the Chinese have been understandably skeptical of most things Christian.

One of the few times that Christianity had impact on the Chinese masses, albeit in a rather contorted form, was during the Tai Ping movement. A peasants' rebellion, led by a Chinese calling himself "the little brother of

▲ *The Empress' phoenix crown in gold, enamel and precious stones, a sample of the great artistic skill of that time.*

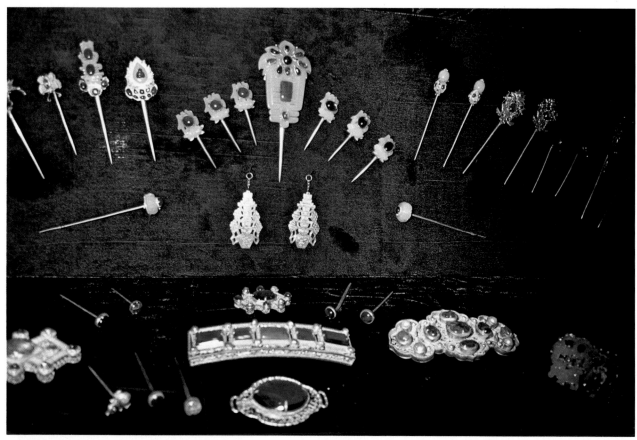

▲ *The Empress carried about fifteen pounds on her head on ceremonial occasions, with her crown and hairpins of jade and gold.*

▲ *Samples of gold coins found together with Wan Li's imperial seal.*

Map of the Ch'ing Dynasty's summer residence, north-west of Peking. An artificial lake, from which the Emperor could reach The Forbidden City by boat, is situated in front of the palace grounds. ▶

▲ *The ornate architecture of the Summer Palace. The pavilion above is made entirely of cast bronze.*

Jesus," conquered a great part of the country and so threatened the regime and the Christian western powers that they united to crush Jesus' little brother and his disciples.

Other great powers—Russia, France, Japan, Germany—competed with the English for the title that the Chinese had given foreigners: "the foreign devils." At the end of the nineteenth century, China was torn apart by "the open door policy," the name given to the foreign policy of the western nations which perpetuated their own high-handed domination of China's sovereign territory and trade. What saved the country may have been distrust of the rapacious and newly-awakened Chinese nationalists. At the turn of the century, a secret patriotic society, The Fists of Right and Harmony, led a popular uprising and punished many missionaries and Chinese Christians for the offences committed by the foreign imperialists. These disturbances are referred to as the Boxer Rebellion.

▲ *During the last days of the corrupt Ch'ing Dynasty, the Dowager Empress ordered this Mississippi River boat, built in marble, for her pleasure.*

▲ *The bedroom of the Empress Tzu-hsi.*

Beautifully decorated promenades like this were built to protect the high sovereign against rain. Much of it was destroyed by the ravages of the Europeans in 1860, when Lord Elgin, the British envoy to Peking, ordered the Chinese Summer Palace to be plundered and burned. ▶

72

◄ *The Dowager Empress Tzu-hsi, in a Chinese painting from the turn of the century. Her sad face shows evidence of the fight she led, to the bitter end, for the continued existence of her dynasty.*

An historic picture, taken by me on an earlier trip, of a small caravan in the last days of the "Silk-way" between Kalgan (today called Chiangchiakou) and Peking. ▼

▲ *This is how an artist imagined the first meeting, in 1274, between the Venetian traveller, Marco Polo, and China's ruler, the Mongol Emperor Kublai Khan. Marco Polo's report of his journeys, and his seventeen-year stay in China, is one of the most extraordinary travel books ever written.*

In 1911, the corrupt empire of the Ch'ing Dynasty was overthrown at last and China became a republic. Its first president was Sun Yat-sen, whose memory is greatly honored in China and elsewhere throughout the world.

▲ *"Give them a fight," was Tzu-hsi's simple order, when European troops tried to reach Peking during the Boxer Rebellion in 1900. Members of the sect I Ho Chuan (The Fists of Right and Harmony) here convey imprisoned "foreign devils" to a summary trial.*

The Sun Yat-sen Mausoleum is situated on a high mountain outside of Nanking. After many unsuccessful attempts, he finally overthrew the decadent empire, and established a republic in 1912.

CHINA'S IMPERIAL DYNASTIES

2183–1751 B.C.	Hsia, (probably legendary)
c. 1766–1123 B.C.	Shang, or Yin
1152–256 B.C.	Chou
221–207 B.C.	Ch'in
202 B.C.–221 A.D.	Han
221–589 A.D.	Six Dynasties
589–618 A.D.	Sui
618–906 A.D.	Tang
907–960 A.D.	Five Dynasties and Ten States
960–1279 A.D.	Sung
1280–1368 A.D.	Yüan
1368–1644 A.D.	Ming
1644–1912 A.D.	Ch'ing

The founder of modern China, Sun Yat-sen, rests here. Even the communists regard him with respect and reverence.

THE REVOLUTION

"We are the only ones who succeeded. The others had their chance, but they failed."

That was the Chinese Communists' answer to the question of why their political system with its harsh discipline was the only possible alternative for China. Liberals and conservatives, reformers and democrats had all failed to correct the chaos which prevailed in the Chinese republic during the first decades after the fall of the empire. The country was torn by constant civil war, and often had competing governments residing in Peking, Nanking, Wuhan and Canton at the same time. Foreign domination of territory and trade continued to be as humiliating as it had been during the empire. The poor were bullied

A column of The Red Army, crossing the Luting bridge, as they had done during the Long March.

81

▲ *The majority of the people often lived in unimaginable misery.*

▲ *Peasants were often bullied by warlords and landowners.*

▲ *There were many strikes and disturbances among the workers in the cities. This painting depicts a riot in the port city of Tientsin, where the hatred of the foreign imperialists was particularly great because of the trade concessions forced upon the people there.*

▲ *Mao Tse-tung was born in the village of Shao Shan, in Hunan province, on December 26, 1893.*

83

by warlords and landowners. Famine and flood claimed hundreds of thousands of victims.

One of the first signs of a national awakening to a radical way of thinking was the May 4th movement. This name was given to the protests and riots of the students in the spring of 1919 against the unfavorable peace terms following the First World War. At about this time a necessary condition for democracy in China began to come about, namely the reorganization and simplification of the Chinese written language. A further sign of the change to come was the formation of the Association of Marxist Studies in Peking in 1918. One of its members was a young unknown farmer's son, Mao Tse-tung.

▲ *The Red Army discipline during the Long March has frequently been used as valuable political propaganda.*

For ten years after the Long March, Mao Tse-tung and the communists had their headquarters in Yenan. ▶

84

▲ *During the early stages of land reform, the landowners were often tried and quickly convicted and punished on the spot by the soldiers and peasants.*

▲ *On August 1, 1927, Chou En-lai led the overwhelming defeat of Chiang Kai-shek's soldiers in the battle at Nanchang. The red flag of China was raised for the first time after that victory.*

For a long time it looked as if the left-wing party, the Kuomintang, founded by Sun Yat-sen and the Russian Borodin, (the principal Soviet advisor to the Kuomintang from 1923 to 1927 was Mikhail Borodin, a former editor of *The Moscow News*), would bring about the dreams of the patriots, the reformers and *even* the communists. In the twenties the Russians, particularly Stalin, pinned their faith on the Kuomintang, in spite of the fact that Mao Tse-tung and his sympathizers had already formed the CPC (Communist Party of China) in July 1921. In 1919 Chou En-lai, who was to become Mao's foremost comrade-in-arms and the first prime minister of Communist China, formed a revolutionary study group in the north, near Tientsin. During this period the power-hungry general Chiang Kai-shek, and the right-wing forces within the Kuomintang, were most influential, and the communists were expelled. By the end of the decade the communists were pursued and massacred, particularly in the big cities. The Communist Party was badly decimated and needed to be reorganized. It turned to the peasant masses in the countryside. From the start, Mao Tse-tung impressed his opinions on the new revolutionary movement. At first he worked in the province of Hunan in the center of China, and later the movement spread to other parts of the country.

The full history, including early strikes, the establishment of the first party cells, and the building of Red bases in western and northern China, comprise an heroic chronicle of martyrdom. For example, of the eighteen original members of the peasants' party, not one escaped Chiang Kai-shek's executioners. Mao's first wife was killed. All but one of the twenty-eight communist bases were liquidated by Kuomintang troops. Only the legendary base in Yenan survived.

Eventually the Reds prevailed, largely because they were supported by the majority of the peasant population. This is illustrated by the story of the Red Army's victory at Lu-ting. The people there said that the souls of dead rebels no longer had to wail and howl in the night, for now they were avenged.

The Long March is widely considered to be the Red Army's most heroic achievement. Despite constant battles with Chiang Kai-shek's well-equipped troops, Mao and his ragamuffin army was able to find haven at last in Yenan in Shensi province after covering some 12,000 miles on foot through merciless terrain, across wild rivers, snow-clad mountains, swamps and wind-blown steppes. All these and the Kuomintang's continual harassment claimed a horrible toll of lives. Some idea of the distance they traveled and the hardships they endured can be gained by imagining a walk from the Arctic Circle through Europe and Africa down to the Cape of Good Hope, without roads, with little food, and with Chiang always in hot pursuit.

The Red leaders contributed to the fighting morale and spirit of self-sacrifice by sharing all of the sacrifices and hardships of their men. At one point Mao became ill and had to be carried on a stretcher over the Big Snow Mountains. In the worst of times, he was able to encourage his soldiers to carry on. An aide tells this story:

"In the middle of August we left Maoeul-kai, where we had stayed for about a month, and started our march over the big swampy steppes. No human being had ever managed to cross them.

"In front of us lay a total wasteland—not the slightest sign of life. Rotting vegetation covered the land on this part of the steppe as far as we could see. We marched on in stinking mud; the eternal sloshing got on our nerves. One false step and you might sink down to your knees in the mud. You even risked drowning in it. Some did. After falling it was as easy to get up as to climb to heaven if no companion were near by to lend a helping hand. More than once, when one of us sank into the sticky muck, it was Chairman Mao who dragged us out with his strong arms.

"It was cold and the weather changed continually. Sometimes it rained, sometimes it snowed, sometimes great hail fell; every step was full of trouble."

"Chairman Mao was always in the lead. Every now and then he would stop and call us, one by one. He would not proceed until everyone had answered. Sometimes, when he saw that our strength was almost at an end, he would tell us funny stories and make us roar with laughter. It helped us forget our weariness.

"Our comrades seldom complained, never expressed displeasure; everyone felt an unconquerable determination. We could *not* be broken. With Chairman Mao with us, we were filled with optimism."

Harsh discipline forbade Red Army soldiers to take *anything* from the civil population without payment. The Long March was not only a triumph for Mao's guerrilla warfare, it was a retreat which became *political* propaganda of the first magnitude.

During the controversy between the Communists and the Kuomintang all of China was engaged in another great struggle for life—against the Japanese, who had invaded and annexed Manchuria in 1931. It was then that Pu-Yi functioned as their puppet-emperor. Subsequently the Japanese attacked mainland China on a large scale. Peking, Tientsin, Shanghai and Nanking were captured, and the Chinese government was forced to withdraw to Hangchou in the west. When it fell, the government people withdrew all the way to Chungking in Szechuan province.

At first, Chiang Kai-shek and the Communists cooperated in resisting the threats from outside. Later, when the Japanese had been defeated by the Allies, ending the Second World War, the final act of the drama of China's modern history unfolded.

In the beginning, Chiang and the Kuomintang enjoyed military superiority, but after three years they were defeated by the Communists. In the spring of 1949, Chiang and his government fled to Taiwan, and on October 1 of that year, at a mass meeting in Peking, Mao Tse-tung proclaimed the People's Republic of China. The Revolution had overcome the odds and had prevailed.

There are many men and women still alive who can describe the time before the Revolution and what that struggle cost those who dedicated their lives to it. In a hotel in Shanghai, I met Chen Hui-ru, a low-voiced little woman, a teacher from the province of Hopeh. My Chinese author-friends introduced me to her when they heard that I was writing a play about the women of China during the Revolution. She told me of her memories of the struggle of the first communist generation, and described their martyrdom and their final victory. It was a strange experience for me to be told the story from the "inside." She had been one of those agitators who, during my Western childhood, had been depicted as scoundrels in so many films and books.

In my play, I called her the "Fourteenth Woman"—or "She Who Sat in the Tiger-Chair." She, of course, did not speak in blank verse, but, apart from that, almost word for word, I quoted in the play what she told me:

◀ *Mao Tse-tung proclaims The Peoples' Republic of China at a mass meeting in the Square of Heavenly Peace, in Peking, on October 1, 1949.*

89

▲ *"She Who Sat in the Tiger Chair"—Chen Hui-ru, the primary teacher from Hopeh.*

▲ *Retired female workers from the textile factory in Shanghai. "Afterwards, they sat down in a semi-circle on the small chairs of the day nursery, and started talking with me. They rested their large work-worn hands on their knees, their faces were lined by age and hard work."*

Mao Tse-tung's principal apartment in the Agricultural Institute at Canton, where he lived in t 1920s while planning the theoretical groundwor for the Revolution. The girl is pointing at a phot of Mao's mother, brothers, and siste In the photo at the right, we ca see his first wife, who wa killed by the Kuo mintang, and his two children.

Choir of old women in a textile factory.

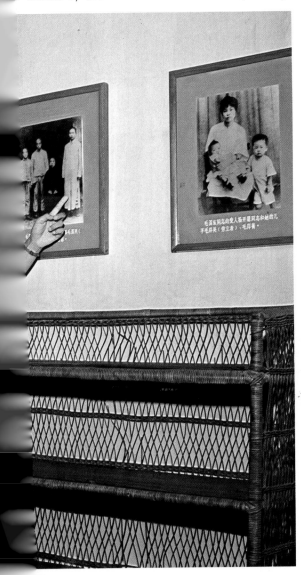

"They tie you to two chairs
with your legs tied together
and resting on the other chair.
Then they put brick after brick on your legs
until the knees buckle the wrong way.
I was in the Tiger-Chair for two hours
and twice I fainted from pain.
But my legs never broke—
I suppose they were softer than my husband's.
When the last battles of Shanghai were raging—
we heard the male prisoners singing happily—
But the same night we saw trucks picking them up . . .
taking them to the Execution-Grounds.
My husband was thirty-nine when they killed him.
He became a communist when he was sixteen.
The next day they gave me his bloody blanket.
I asked to be allowed to give it to our children—
should I die.
My comrades bribed the jailer
and he agreed.
The children had been suffering.
The oldest one had burned his face
when they were trying to boil vegetables—
They were so young.
None of our neighbors dared to help them
because the house was watched by Chiang's soldiers.
They didn't understand why their father
no longer needed his blanket—
and I didn't have the heart to tell them.
It was raining and I watched them leave with the blanket.
The next day they came back
and talked about their father as if he was alive.
Everybody in my cell cried
until the jailer came and shut us up with his whip.
The night before the liberation of Shanghai
we all prepared to die—
but before our jailers had time to kill us
we smashed the iron gates with stones
and broke out.
It was May 27 . . .
When I came home
I immediately started to search for my husband's dead body.
On June 20 I found him—
I must have turned over ten thousand bodies.
Then, for the first time, I realized
what sacrifices the Revolution demands
and what my husband meant when he said:
'the Revolution must go through our hearts like a sword.' "

"I started working in the factory when I was only seven years old. I went barefoot simply because I had no shoes. In winter I left my home while it was still dark and I returned home after it had turned dark again. Almost every day, I saw in the streets the corpses of people who had frozen to death, mostly children and old people. I never went to school and never learned to read. At our place of work, if anyone became sick he was fired at once. Anyone unfortunate enough to have no relatives was forced to beg or starve."

"I started working in the silk-weaving mill when I was nine. We worked sixteen hours a day and almost never saw the sun. I married while young and had fourteen children. Five of them survived, the rest died. I was forced to sell two—one of them to a family on a boat. I have no idea where he is or even if he is still alive."

"I have had ten children, but famine, disease and flood took nine of them. Sometimes my husband and I had work in the cotton factory, which was owned by some wealthy English ladies; but most of the time we were out of work and were reduced to begging.

"Once both of us were offered work in the factory. We did not have anyone who could take care of our newborn baby, so we smuggled it inside under some rags in a basket, hoping it would keep quiet. But very soon it started screaming and we were both fired. The child starved to death because I did not have any milk. Afterwards, I nearly went mad and wanted to return with the dead baby in the basket to place it outside the mill, but my husband stopped me.

"Only one of my many children ever reached full adulthood. She was a girl and has given me two grandchildren. I am holding one of them in my arms right now. My daughter is working in the factory and I am caring for the children for her. I am quite happy now. The factory is no longer owned by the English ladies."

All of the above I heard from old, pensioned, female workers in a textile factory in Shanghai as they told me about their lives. This was no carefully produced propaganda show. The old ladies were all speaking at the same time, and my interpreter could not always follow. Many of them cried as their memories overwhelmed them. Even I couldn't keep back my tears. What they told me is a slice of living history. I remember,

BEFORE AND AFTER

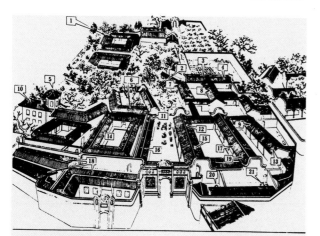

The Criminal Country Estate

1. Courtyard where charges were collected
2. Summer rooms for opium smoking
3. Stock room for grain
4. Basement prison cell, partly filled with water for torturing peasants
5. Summer house
6. Stock room
7. Banquet hall
8. Buddhist prayer room
9. Third opium room
10. Boudoir
11. Collection office
12. Living room (Chinese style)
13. Ladies' guest room
14. Official residences
15. Living room (Western style)
16. Reception room for secret society plotters
17. Liu Wen-tai's bedroom
18. Stock room for grain
19. Second opium room
20. Servants' well
21. Master's and mistresses' well

▲ *A tenant farmer's old wife on her way to the weigh-station with her grain.*

◀ *The shocking scenes depicted in the clay tablets on this page took place on this country estate.*

during my childhood, reading in the papers about hundreds of thousands of Chinese who drowned when the Yang-tze-kiang or the Yellow River flooded, and when the province of Shansi or Hopeh was hit by drought or famine. But that was much too far away and the numbers were too large to have had any reality for me. All those tragedies were dry statistics. Here, in the factory, in Shanghai, I realized for the first time that these incomprehensible catastrophies affected *real* people. These old women still carry marks on their bodies and in their souls. I didn't smile cynically when the "Old Women's Choir" started singing its simple songs about how happy they are now that Mao's sun has risen.

There are about forty members in the choir—old worn workers with gnarled faces. Almost every one of them has memories of the hard times before the Revolution, but they all affirm that things *are* different now. The ancient ghost of starvation has been quelled for the first time in recallable history. Families don't have to sell their children any longer. All young people learn to read and write (of these forty old women, only *one* can write). The children are taken care of by their grandparents or in well-managed day nurseries while their parents are working, and there are doctors and medicines for the sick.

I ought not to be so impressed. We have achieved about the same thing in my country.

A little more than a hundred years ago the same poor also had starved to death in Sweden. Some were forced to sell *their* children. Our last big famine occurred as recently as 1868.

What makes people marvel about the "Chinese Wonder" is that the Chinese made this dramatic change from a starving underdeveloped country to material security and human dignity in just *one* decade. Until 1949, the people were subjugated in misery and humiliation by domestic and foreign oppressors. In the parks of Shanghai during the forties were signs saying: "Entrance forbidden to Chinese and dogs."

Wherever you go in China you will hear tales of the past similar to those I heard in the textile factory in Shanghai. There are still many people who have experienced the two eras—before the revolution and after the revolution—two expressions that the traveler will hear over and over again. The communist regime is doing its best to keep the contrasts fresh in everyone's mind. One of the most harrowing testimonies to the change is the exhibition of sculptures which was sent around China in the sixties. It was called the "Tenant Farm," and described the life of a poor tenant farmer's family and the conditions of the day laborers before the Revolution. There were more than one hundred life-size sculptures made of straw and dried clay, the poor man's marble.

The despotic landowner being dragged off by Red Army soldiers. ▼

▲ *Before the Revolution, life for the small, privileged upper class was idyllic.*

This lake is situated in a wonderfully beautiful countryside at Hangchou. It was much appreciated by the imperial courts, and by Marco Polo, who described it lyrically.

MAO TSE-TUNG

Mao Tse-tung was born on December 26, 1893 in the small village of Shao Shan in the province of Hunan. His father, Mao Jen-cheng, had a small farm of only two acres. The house had a dirt floor, a thatched roof, the food was plain. In spite of Spartan fare, Mao grew to be tall and sturdy. His historic achievement was in part due to his abundunt mental and physical stamina.

At the age of seven, he entered the village school. He was a talented pupil and had an obstinate character which stayed with him throughout his school years. In all of the schools he attended, he led strikes and uprisings. The passion to reform the schools lasted all of his life. "Why *not* sleep during a *boring* lesson?" he often asked even in his late years. At an early age he began to disagree with his father, though he continued to be deeply attached to his mother, Wen Chi-mei. Sympathy for the oppressed women of China was one of the continuing themes of his life interest, as was his special sympathy for the poor farmers in his home province, who early on had unsuccessfully attempted to revolt against the authorities and the landowners.

At the age of thirteen, Mao had to leave school to work on his father's farm. He continued his interest in reading, nonetheless. Two years later he married a girl five years his senior. The marriage was never consummated. In the following year, Mao left his native village and resumed his studies, first in an intermediate school and then at the Institute in the capital of his province. When the revolution of 1911 broke out, he joined the republicans. As a sign of independence he cut off his own hateful pigtail and those of his close friends because they represented a sign of Manchurian domination.

During the years that followed he spent his time in study and in politics. In 1917, he became a librarian in Peking. It was then that he had his first contact with communism. He met his first true wife, Yang Kai-hui, in 1919. That was a love match that was related in their minds to the new revolutionary spirit.

In 1921 Mao and others of like mind founded the Communist Party of China. From that time on his personal life was almost identical with the course of the Chinese Revolution. He lived his life for the party with all the intensity his soul could muster, and shared all the suffering and victories of the Revolution.

He and Yang Kai-hui had two sons. One of them was killed in the Korean War in 1950, the other is still working in a People's Commune. Mao's wife was captured in 1939 by the Kuomintang and was tortured and assassinated. The same fate befell Mao's sister. With his second wife, Hu Tzu-chen, he had three children. Two of them were left with a farmer during the Long March and were never identified again. That marriage ended in divorce. Mao's third wife, actress Chiang Chin, was prominent in the cultural revolution and until recently was one of the leading powers in the radical left wing of the party.

Until his death at the age of 82, Mao's influence on the political thought of China was primal and continuing. He died on September 9, 1976; his thoughts are still alive.

◀ *Occasionally, Mao-Tse-tung would withdraw to one of the lovely mountain districts in the middle of China. Almost all of his later poems were written there. It is strange that this modern revolutionary wrote in the style of the Tang period, which was more than a thousand years before his time.*

A RICH WELL FULL OF WATER

"We live in a People's Commune."

To western ears this might sound like a fate worse than death. People's Commune, that must mean children taken away from parents to be brought up in collectives, brainwashing and constant military drill, never a corner of your own, men and women in separate barracks, families scattered, in short, the robot society at its *worst*.

I was brainwashed, but *not* by the Chinese. After I arrived in China, I was invited to the People's Commune Haitin, west of Peking. There I found the standard of living quite low, compared to western life, but I saw neither military police nor separation of men and women in barracks.

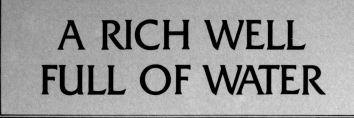

For 3,000 years the water buffalo has been used as a draft animal by the Chinese peasant. With its broad cloven hoofs, it can easily walk through the muddy rice fields.

▲ *This sketch shows the People's Commune Lei-Liu, in Kwangtung province.*

Here are portions of some of the things they told me. "Our families live together. Ten families live in this house, one family in each room. We share the same kitchen. We have electric light—next year we will get a gas stove, maybe."

"Before the Revolution we lived with three families in one room. It was much worse. We lived on cabbage and rice all year round when we could get it. We often went hungry. One wealthy man owned the whole area around here. I, myself, was often beaten by him."

Four or five people in a room fifteen by eighteen feet. Ten families sharing a small kitchen with a coal-burning stove. Is this something to be so immensely proud of? Something which the outside world often calls the "Chinese Wonder?"

One again I realized that you cannot understand the new China if you do not consider her background. Only a few years ago they lived on a lower level than did the poorest in the western countries at the beginning of the 19th century. Large parts of the country lived in conditions similar to those of our Middle Ages.

When the communists came to power in 1949, utter chaos racked all of China, with its 600 million inhabitants. The country had been devastated by invasion and civil war, famine raged and hardly any industry existed in the disintegrating country.

Eight-five to ninety percent of the population were farmers. Consequently, the new regime found it difficult to follow the form of *classic* communism, in which the industrial workers of the cities lead the revolution. Mao Tse-tung had to develop an agrarian variation of the classic ideas of Marx and Lenin—a variation which has since become the prototype for other revolutionary movements in other underdeveloped countries. One of the first programs was land reform. Chinese arable

▲ *Intensive irrigation guarantees harvests of many crops including bananas and sugar cane.*

▲ *A small power station maintains the water level between two systems. Here small boats and cargo-sampans are passing through the locks.*

▲ *Brick and tile are the principal building materials in the villages of southern China.*

▲ *In picturesque barges equipped with cabins, fish are kept alive for transportation to the nearest city. The trip may take a week.*

▲ *Edible fish cultivation in small village ponds is a factor of great economic importance. Fishermen go into the water to draw their nets and bring in the catch.*

land was divided into more than one hundred million small plots whose ownership was given to the people.

After the first enthusiasm they realized that so many small units were economically unsound. They could never utilize the industrial equipment needed to lower the cost of food and grow more of it. A self supporting agriculture had to be developed if industrial expansion was to follow.

Then they experimented with small scale cooperatives, but at the end of the fifties the step was finally taken to develop People's Communes of thousands of members each. The one in Haitin, for example, has 3,300 households and 14,000 people. There are some which are ten times as large. In the mountains and in the desert areas they are usually much smaller.

▲ *Silkworms are grown in low huts with thatched roofs.*

▲ *The insignificant silk-spinner, the silkworm.*

▲ *Caterpillars hatch in a few days in the damp heat of the huts.*

▲ *As the caterpillars grow, they ravenously consume the juicy mulberry leaves.*

◄ *Here the finished silk cocoons, which contain a thread more than half a mile long, are being picked.*

This machine, constructed by the farmers of Lei-Liu Commune, catches the beginning of the thread and unwinds the thin silk. ▼

In the People's Commune's own embroidery factory, beautiful tablecloths, with bird and flower motifs, are produced. ▼

The warm water of the canal offers a pleasant spot in which the small children of the People's Commune can play. ▼

The People's Communes are their way of organizing the society into large effective production units with industries, farms, day nurseries, schools and homes for the aged, all under a single management which is elected by the people who live in them.

Nowadays there are more than 75,000 People's Communes in China. They are totally socialistic and deliver their entire output to the state. Once the problems of the change-over to the new system of communal cooperation were solved, production in-

The small homes of the farmers are quite simply furnished, yet they are well suited to their purpose. In southern China, a family meal often consists of fish, boiled rice and fried vegetables. ▶

▲ A small cargo-sampan is delivering sand to a building site. The boat's sails have been stowed to one side.

▲ A tributary of the Hsi Si-kiang river runs north-west of Lei-Liu, and connects with the road to Canton.

▲ *Good hygiene is carefully observed. Toward evening children and their mothers gather in the baths to wash and shower.*

▲ *A young schoolteacher instructing her class in the steps of the difficult "rubber band dance."*

Sampans and small boats on the Pearl River in Canton. The old river people, who were born and lived and died on their boats, have moved ashore, to a more comfortable life.

creased without interruption. The yield per acre increased six-fold for cereals and cotton, and the cultivated area was enlarged by 10,000 to 20,000 acres annually. For the Chinese, there is no stronger argument for their system than that they, unlike all others before them, have conquered their ancient enemy —hunger.

Chinese industrial production has recently risen 10–15 per cent each year, and the standard of living has gone up on farms and in homes. Every other family now seems able to afford a bicycle and a radio, but getting these things stills demands a lot of hard work and thrift. Generally a laborer earns 80–100 yuan a month (about $40–$50), and a bicycle costs slightly over 150 yuan, or two months' pay.

In 1959 China was struck by the worst and longest drought in its history. In spite of all, there were no deaths from starvation during that difficult time. China can now supply its enormous population with the cereal grains she needs. From 1949 to 1973 production rose from 110 million tons to more than 250 million tons per year.

Thus the agricultural People's Communes form the basis of China's economy, but the People's Communes are not only to make agriculture more efficient. They are also

The noodles are hung on bamboo canes. When dry, they are packed in bundles to be cooked in soup. ▶

112

Men and women work side by side on the farms. A basket of sweet potatoes like this weighs more than 65 pounds. The monthly pay is about 40 yuan (about $20.00). ▼

These molds are called "Cheeses" and are made from potato flour. After baking in the sun they are cut into long thin strips called "noodles." ▼

▲ *In summer the small farm building at the left is used as a kitchen and wash house.*

▲ *The most important feature of a north Chinese home is the broad cement bed, under which they can build a fire. It is called a "kang", and is large enough for several people.*

responsible for developing much of the nation's industry, its cultural life, its educational system, its health progress, and its military defense.

China is also endeavoring to decentralize so that each People's Commune should be as nearly self-supporting as possible. It should provide not only food, but all the necessities of life, including those of the spirit. It is not difficult to imagine what strength such self-supporting units can give a country's military defense.

Decentralization aims to wipe out the difference between rural and urban areas. Unlike westerners, the Chinese fear the danger of unchecked urbanization. They contend that the privileges of higher living standards and better education should not be available to the urban population only. The new society being planned in China will try to prevent overly populated and densely built areas.

Even though all People's Communes are run according to the same general principles and have the same ideals, in a country as large as China, they differ widely. Haitin could have been as isolated as a Middle-European peasants' village. In the People's Commune of the

---

▲ *Four generations—formerly a very rare picture in China where the average life span was much shorter than it is today.*

▲ *A typical country shop in 1976. When People's Communes were formed, they offered improved services to the farmers through their shops, cottage hospitals, etc.*

▲ *Duck farming is common in the countryside. Here in the People's Commune of Chuang-Chia, 40,000 ducks are raised each year.*

▲ *"Peking duck" is a delicacy in many Chinese restaurants. The ducks are force-fed to develop the best flavor.*

▲ *Chuang-Chia has nineteen elementary schools and six middle schools. This is a lesson in elementary geography.*

▲ *Sports have come to the countryside. Each week a league game is played between members of different work teams from the commune.*

116

▲ *Tachai is located on the dry loess-plateau in Shansi province. When I first visited here, it was like walking on the moon. How could anyone cultivate anything here? Great parts of the older terrace plantations had been destroyed, and the earth washed away by terrible storms.*

▲ *Newly-built dwellings for the Tachai production brigade are situated in a hollow between the loess mountains.*

Only fifteen years ago, many farmers lived in caves. Today they make their own brick, for the building of homes, schoolhouses, cottage hospitals and places of business. ▶

Tiger Hill, some four hundred miles further south, the climate is warmer. They produce rice, tea, and citrus fruits. While I was there, I was shown around by the superintendent, Chu Hung-li, a small man as spry as a squirrel with his hair all on end.

"We used to have a proverb here that there are three knives which cut the farmer's head: starvation, the land-owner and the imperial sheriffs. Now we have gotten rid of all three. This People's Commune was founded in 1958, but the farmers had already joined together in a cooperative several years before that."

He showered me with figures while we walked between greenhouses and past steaming fertilizer mounds.

"Thirteen thousand of us live here. There are still five People's Communes of the same size near Suchou. When we started, these farms produced 30 kins of wheat and 400 kins of rice. Last year we harvested 210 kins of wheat and 854 kins of rice."

I had no idea how much a kin was—I later found that it's about 132 pounds—but the increase sounded quite imposing. I asked about something more interesting to a town-dweller like me.

"Are those who live here allowed to have any property of their own?"

"Of course, why shouldn't we? Three hundred of our three thousand families have been able to buy their own radios."

He was evidently very proud of this fact—that every tenth family could afford a radio. You must remember how they had lived before. In 1965 not a single tractor, not a single truck could be found on this enormous farm.

"We have oxen and buffalos to pull plows and use as draft animals." And the thing he was most proud of, "We have fourteen elementary schools in our People's Commune!"

Stone blocks are cut into smaller pieces, so that men can carry them up to the terraces. ▶

118

They dig material by hand from a gravel pit to edge the plantation terraces.

Chen Yung-kuei was the man who—more than anybody else—inspired the people to rebuild Tachai after the catastrophe in 1963. When this picture was taken in 1966, he told me that they had already built 42 miles of paved terraces.

▲ *These girls are nationally famous in China for their personal sacrifices and model achievements in farming in Tachai.*

▲ *At the end of the last century, Shansi province was hit by one of the worst famines in history. Almost ten million people died. Today starvation is nearly eradicated, and due to irrigation and terraced plantations, impressive harvests are common.*

▲ *The secret behind their success is fine teamwork, good leadership and faith in their own ability. "To learn from Tachai" is a slogan which may be applied to all of Chinese agriculture. Chen Yung-kuei is a member of the Central Committee of the Communist Party and a minister in the government.*

A farmer's wife, shopping in a well-stocked store in Tachai. ▼

▲ *Cattle on their way to the People's Commune "Rich Well Full of Water" in Inner Mongolia.*

◄ *Cultivation of corn and wheat have done best here. Everything demands meticulous care in this climate, where it only rains once or twice a year. Here wheat is being thinned by hand, and tender shoots can be seen in the foreground.*

A Mongolian shepherdess.

▲ *Some of the 78,000 animals of the People's Commune, with their shepherds.*

▲ *A descendant of Atilla the Hun and Genghis Khan.*

▲ *Large herds of camel are everywhere in this commune, which is at about the same latitude as Rome.*

Banquet in a "yurt," or Mongolian tent. They don't have much furniture. ▶

◄ *"Their dwellings are white woolen tents,
bound with black ropes over a loose
framework of woven sticks."*

I met some workers at a commune in
Tachai, in Shansi province. They rubbed the
clay off their hands and came up to us, grin-
ning. At their home, they all served us so
much tea that my tummy felt like a drum.
The poorest of them served hot water. The
Chinese call this "white tea."

"The poorest?" you wonder. "What sort of
communism is that? Are they not all exactly
alike?"

No, not exactly alike. Even in a People's
Commune, a diligent man might work under
better conditions than a lazy one. If he is a
thrifty person, he can put money in a bank and
accumulate enough for a bicycle, a watch or a
radio; but he cannot buy land and use other
men as day laborers, or own a factory, where
the work of others might be exploited.
However, a certain degree of private ownership is allowed—perhaps a garden, or pigs or
chickens.

Chi Leng-sen was one of those who has
worked hard and saved to make his life better.
He had a cottage with four rooms and a
kitchen, all for himself—and six children and
the grandparents.

"We used to live nearby. We had ten
people in one room."

His new house was very simple. The
ground floor was stone. There were plain
hand-made wooden tables and stools like
those in an old homestead or in pioneer country. But Chi, family father and owner of his
own house in Kiangsu, was clean and honest.
We chatted spontaneously and when I left,
with a big smile full of humor and understanding, he pressed my hand and said "goodbye." I
no longer believe Kipling's phrase that East
and West shall never meet. I think they have
met, as Chi and I have.

◄ *Pupils outside their schoolhouse.*

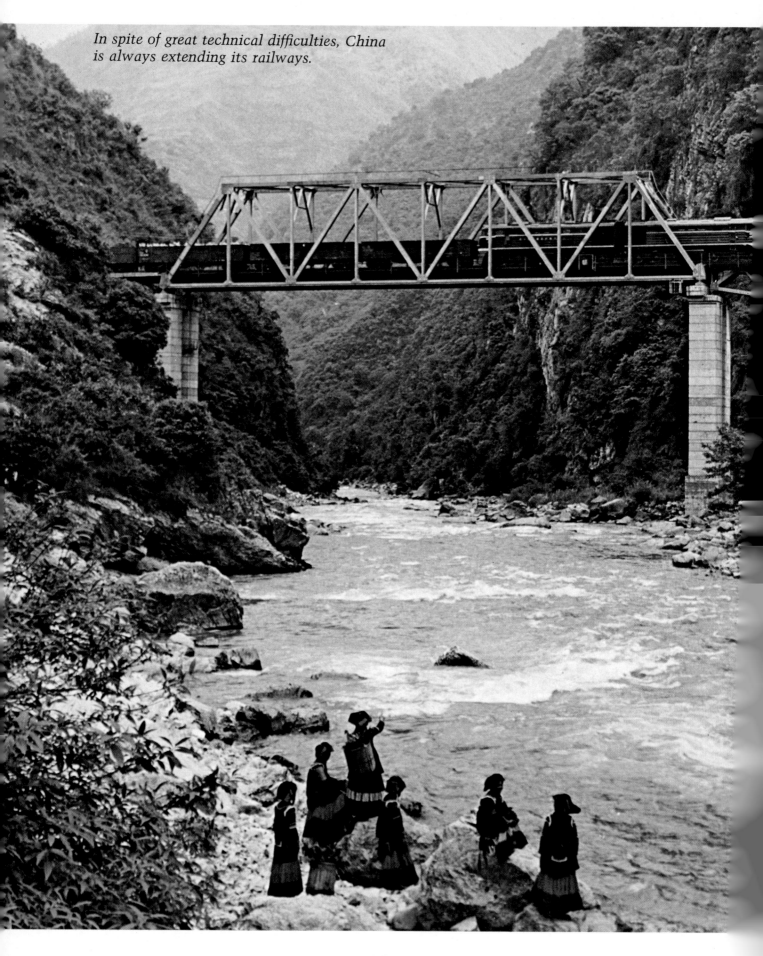

In spite of great technical difficulties, China is always extending its railways.

◀ River crossings have always been bottlenecks to traffic. Up to only a few years ago, the railway over the Yang-tze-kiang had to be ferried across the river.

◀ The steelworks of Wuhan was to produce the girders to build the bridge over the Yang-tze-kiang at Nanking. However, production was interrupted when Russian technicians were called back home. The Chinese have never forgiven the Russians for this action and that is one of the causes of the present conflict between them.

◀ An artist sketches a demonstration at the steelworks.

◀ The steel which the Russians delivered for the bridge was faulty, so the industrial workers decided that the large steelworks in Anshan should make the necessary girders.

127

▲ *In* 1968 *after eight years' work, the bridge was finished. It was built on two levels: an upper level for automobile traffic, and a lower one for the railroad.*

Building the bridge was a test of the strength of their "own ability," and the most successful industrial project of the Cultural Revolution. The 4.2 mile long construction, spanning about a mile of open water, required an heroic contribution from divers, among others. The Yang-tze-kiang is about 130 feet deep at this point. In order to anchor the bridge foundations to the river bottom, the divers had to blast about 98 feet of sand. Because of the bridge, the river crossing has been shortened from hours to minutes.

I arrived in Silinhot on the outskirts of the Gobi desert in a small, bumpy airplane. From Silinhot, we went by jeep on a roller coaster road out into the yellow-brown treeless waste, to the People's Commune, Bai Yua Boli Gu. The name means "Rich Well Full of Water." Here eight hundred Mongolian nomads live with their 78,000 animals: camels, horses, cows, sheep. They cultivate practically nothing, but migrate four times a year to new graz-ing grounds for their animals. Their dwellings are white woolen tents bound onto loose frames of woven sticks. There are no other buildings in the village except a few low, one-story sheds. One of these is a school.

Both men and women wear boots, with shirts down to their knees and gaudy silk belts around their waists. In each hut I visited—and there were quite a few—I was invited to have some wine made of fermented milk,

▲ Today in the new China, the use of rickshas is forbidden. One man should not have to pull another. Instead, they use a three-wheeler, called a pedicab. This picture was taken early in the morning on Chang-an, the main street of Peking.

▲ Improving housing is of vital importance to raising the living standards, yet many people still live in inferior houses.

▲ Increasing auto traffic in the cities requires traffic lights and warning lights.

No private automobiles exist in China. Taxicabs, owned by the towns, are available for visitors at all the large hotels. ▼

▲ *A former beggar and his dwelling in what was a slum area in Shanghai. Today the hut is a relic to remind the younger generation of the struggles of its elders.*

▲ *New apartment houses in Shanghai in a former slum area called Lane.*

A steady stream of more than 2 million cyclists flows down the main street as they go to work in the capital.

▲ *Lane, the former slum area, is more than a housing project. In it you will find a well-equipped home industry. Locating industry close to homes is an important consideration in newly built towns.*

▲ *The first display items in radio stores were copies of older European models.*

▲ *Today one finds transistorized sets from all over the world.*

132

with cakes and big fatty pieces of newly-slaughtered lamb. I consequently feared the journey home in the jeep.

The conversation here is slow. Since the Mongolian language is incomprehensible even to the Chinese, everything must be interpreted from Mongolian to Chinese, and then reinterpreted from Chinese to English. Even the written characters in the temples of Silinhot and Huhehot are different from the Chinese.

It is difficult to imagine greater contrasts than those between the living conditions of the small tribe of nomads in "Rich Well Full of Water" in Inner Mongolia, and those prevailing at the much larger sub-tropical commune, Tiger Hill. But the political and economic systems are the same, and the speeches which the chairman of each community made about "before the liberation" and "after the liberation" in both places were the same to me.

▲ *There is no mistaking the popularity of the bicycle. It costs about $50.00, and in China the cyclist can still leave his machine unlocked. Chinese do not steal from each other. Many western tourists have testified that theft is as unlikely as making the Chinese accept tips.*

"Twelve on one cycle."

The first commercially made status symbol a Chinese family buys is a thermos bottle. Then, after a long hard period of working and saving, they may buy a wrist watch, a radio, a sewing machine or a bicycle. In the streets of Peking and Nanking there are literally millions of bicycles, and the few cars maneuver among them like clumsy crocodiles in a river.

The materialistic standards of our consumption-oriented society, where possessing things nearly runs away with us, and where almost all families have a car and a TV set, where every other teenager owns a tape deck, can hardly be compared to the standards of the Chinese. They, like the Russians, had to meet the demands of heavy industry before even thinking of consumer goods. Trucks, tractors, excavators, railway engines, and machine tools were needed to establish productive, stable farms, mines, dams and power plants.

And, as in the Soviet Union, the Chinese tried to bring about their ambitions with the help of five-year plans. The first of these covered the years 1953–58. It combined a number of campaigns: land reform and reclamation, conversion to a socialist economy, abolition of illiteracy, and women's liberation.

TWELVE
ON ONE CYCLE

The most important of these changes was moral and idealistic, and resulted in what I like to call the "Chinese Wonder." In a couple of decades, corruption, prostitution, opium-abuse and domination by gangsters have been abolished. Now, instead, the Chinese feel pride in their work, a spirit of self-sacrifice, a sence of unity with the state and the Communist Party, and an almost Puritan ethic. Western observers, whether they are friends or enemies, businessmen or tourists, unanimously praise the honesty of the Chinese. I am not the only person who has lost a handkerchief and found it forwarded to my next hotel, washed and ironed, or who has had a tip returned with a message: "You probably forgot this on your table yesterday."

The explanation probably lies in the overwhelming support of the people for the ideals of the communist regime. In the past, there had been opposition. In the fifties, the party used strong measures and liquidated hundreds of thousands of "class enemies" in an "equalization movement." When I visited the central prison in Shanghai, almost sixty per cent of the inmates were political criminals. This would be an incredibly high percen-

Shanghai is the largest city in China. In 1958
the population was about 10 million people;
today it is probably about 13 million. The
Huang-p'u River forms a natural harbor for
ocean-going ships. The high-rise buildings
originated in the period when foreign trade
concessions were forced upon China.

tage in our society, but it is probably the result of the Cultural Revolution at the end of the sixties. Now, after Mao's death, there is conflict between the radical elements of the communist party, centered around Mao's widow, Chiang Ching, and the moderate elements represented by Teng Hsiao. Soon there may be an open struggle for power between them, but it's too early to tell.

But *whatever* price may have been paid for all the splendid "Boy Scout" morality and civic cooperation, the result is still miraculous in view of the *background*. Before the Revolution, the giant city of Shanghai was a world-famous den of iniquity and human degradation. Today pleasure-seeking sailors and tourists cannot find anything more sinful than a game of ping pong.

In their first five-year plan, the Chinese concentrated mostly on heavy industry. With the technical and economic help of the Soviet Union, production increased by no less than nineteen per cent per year.

The second five-year plan, from 1958–63, began with a tremendous national effort which has been called the Great Leap Forward. Its purpose was to decentralize industry and build innumerable small blast-furnaces, factories and mills which could provide local farmers with the products they needed.

Unfortunately, the Great Leap stumbled because of natural catastrophes, and because the Russians suddenly refused to continue their help and cooperation. In 1961, ten thousand Soviet experts left the Chinese factories and industrial projects almost over-

▲ *Harbor traffic in* 1962.

▲ *The same picture in* 1976. *The harbor is used every year by ships from* 80 *foreign countries.*

◄ *Loading and unloading with the help of sampans is no longer a common sight.*

China has started building ships suitable for container traffic. ▼

▲ *About 55% of China's export trade passes through Shanghai harbor. They have large cranes and a modern system of docks. The harbor is continually being extended.*

night, taking with them all their know-how, plans and specifications. The results were almost disastrous. The Chinese have never forgiven the Russians for this betrayal. The conflict which caused the rift was mainly ideological, originating in the Russian fear of and skepticism toward the Chinese brand of communism.

During later five-year plans, China once more strove toward its ambitions and has developed much that is imposing in its industry. At the same time the standard of living within the country has greatly increased. The sale of bicycles and textiles during the years 1974–75 rose by 8%. Radio sales rose 62% and cameras 168%! Within the party, the leaders are beginning to fear that the people will become so bourgeois that they will forget the "constant revolution." A huge permanent industrial exhibition in Shanghai demonstrates not only the most important basic products, but also advances in science and technology, from the hydrogen bomb to heart and lung machines—and even such exotic things as synthetic insulin, which China produced before any other country.

The march of industry during these decades is the result not only of centrally-organized planning, clever politics, and propaganda, but also, and above all, of the cooperation of millions of enthusiastic individuals

"Made in China," *prototype of a modern private car.* ▼

▲ *Shanghai has very advanced textile mills.*

Checking turbine wheels in a heating plant. This picture illustrates a working principle of the new industry: three in one, meaning a team of engineer, scientist and student. ▶

▲ *Machinery hall in the Permanent Industrial Exhibition of Shanghai.*

with high working morale. Gunnar Myrdal, in his book *Asiatic Drama*, considers this the only solution to the problems of the under-developed countries. It is not only help from the outside that poor countries need. Far more important is ideological and moral inspiration which can diminish apathy and corruption at home.

I have heard many imposing statistics on China's industrial development, but none has shown me more about the Great Leap Forward than my visit to a small, primitive shoe polish factory in Taiyuan, the capital of Shansi province. This so called factory consisted of about twenty low ramshackle houses and some very primitive equipment. While I was there, it employed 34 middle-aged women from the city.

"There were eleven of us when we started in 1959. Ignorant housewives, all of us. Only two of us could read—barely."

"But why a shoe polish factory?" I asked.

"We wanted to help in the Great Leap Forward. Our purpose was to serve, not earn, like Chairman Mao says in 'To serve the people.' We tried other products first—candles and moth balls made of waste from nearby factories. But that didn't work out so well. Then we started experimenting with shoe polish. That wasn't very easy either, in the beginning."

"But how did you get this place, and the necessary capital?"

"We built the factory with our own hands. We collected the bricks from the old city wall. It had been smashed. One of us was taught by a carpenter for twelve days and after that, she made all our chairs and benches! And the money . . . you know, those male 'experts' told us that we couldn't do anything without an

initial capital of at least twenty thousand yuan ($10,000). But because we didn't want to borrow any money, even if we could have, we didn't have more than fourteen hundred yuan ($700) to start with."

These were some of their memories as they sat on wooden benches in the factory yard during the dinner hour, dressed in blue trousers, richly colored cotton blouses and black cloth shoes with white soles, laughing at themselves and their past difficulties.

"Here in the city there were jokes and even a song about us. They said our candles were bent and our shoe polish would turn into water. In the beginning they were probably right. We had to wash clothes that were ruined because our shoe polish leaked out of the cans. After almost six hundred experiments, we finally succeeded. By then no one wanted to buy from us. We had to go into the streets and polish shoes for nothing to convince people that our product was good. Now we have a

working capital of nineteen thousand yuan ($9,500) in the bank, we have more than twenty buildings, and we're selling shoe polish to many countries in the socialist world—for example, Rumania, Ghana, Sudan, Guinea."

Of course this may sound like a Chinese Sunday School story, but I find it difficult to imagine these reliable female workers telling me anything but the truth. They weren't trained propagandists.

I saw an outstanding acrobatic troupe in a theatre in Taiyuan. In one of the acts, twelve men rode on one bicycle. They symbolized for me what may be the most important components of the "Chinese Wonder": team morale, willingness to sacrifice luxury, and common ideology. Twelve on one cycle.

▲ *Guiling—a Chinese robot which can handle and choose between about* 60 *different tools.*

One of the thirty women who made the Long March, Ten Ying-chao, tells the story:

"The women who joined the Long March were as persevering and brave as the men. In the First Frontal Army there were thirty women. All of them had taken part in the Revolution, and several had high posts. The Communist Party decided that they should make the Long March. The strongest of them carried their own sleeping-bags and flour rations. During the whole trek they were in high spirits and kept up with the others. As soon as the troops stopped to rest, they took the opportunity to propagandize the local inhabitants, to care for the sick and the wounded, or to cook. They were good examples of revolutionary will-power, optimism and perseverance in spite of difficulties. One of them, Comrade Kang Ke-ching, was a political worker in the Red Army. She wore an army uniform and straw sandals, carried a rifle and marched with the other soldiers.

"All the female comrades stuck it out. None of them deserted and none died along the way. They all reached the end.

"During the Long March I suffered from tuberculosis. The comrades took every possible care of me. There are people who can't believe that a person as sick as I was could march under such difficult circumstances, but I did. Oddly enough, when the March ended I was cured without any special medical treatment despite all the hardships and difficulties."

During the war with Japan and also the civil war against the Kuomintang, both Red Army and the guerrilla women did fight side by side with the men. This was important to the liberation of women in China. It would have been impossible for these women, who had proven their ability and courage in partisan warfare, to return to the traditional role of the household drudge.

Before the Revolution, the lot of Chinese women was pitiable. They had no rights of their own. They were sold like cattle on the marriage market, and they were forced to submit to ancient and barbaric customs. If the family was poor, it was quite common for newborn girls to be killed or sold for a couple of silver dollars. The custom of binding the feet of upper-class girls continued even after Sun Yat-sen's revolution in 1911, and you can still see old grandmothers hobbling about on

350 MILLION WOMEN BECOME HUMAN BEINGS

▲ *"Never have I seen so many marching women as in Asia."*

▲ *Care and skill are characteristic of the younger generation of female technicians, who are doing increasingly more important tasks in industry.*

deformed stumps of feet. The very few women who worked in a profession outside the home or farm received a salary of one-third of what men earned for the very same work. The feeling that women were of much lower value than men stemmed from an old Confucian maxim:

"Women and slaves are hard to treat."

"The woman ought to devote herself to pleasing the man." K'ung Fu-tzu's (Confucius) three rules of obedience all prescribed that the woman be obedient: to her father, to her elder brothers while she was young, to her husband when she married, and to her sons if she became widowed. Thus, from the cradle to the grave, she was to obey *men.*

In a society of this type, prostitution became a frequent means of livelihood for women. In the upper classes, concubines were common. The emperor kept several hundred official mistresses and concubines, and he was the model for all successful men. The famous empress Tzu-hsi, who governed China for several decades at the end of the nineteenth century, started her career as an imperial concubine.

Of course a young girl in old China was never allowed to choose her husband. Often she was married as a child. In times of need, the poor were often forced to sell their wives as well as their daughters to brothels. The story of the "Sixth Woman" in my play, *The Women of Shanghai,* is not invented. It was based on a true story told to me:

"My husband put his mark
on some sort of a contract.
It said that the brothel
would let me go after two years—
and he believed it, poor man.
He really loved me—
even if you don't think so.
But what were we to do
after the terrible drought?
Two of our children were still alive.
One had died of starvation
and one had frozen to death
on the ice-cold 'kang'
where she had once been born.
My worn beauty
was the family's only asset.
The woman-buyer who came to our town
depicted eloquently
how I would be able to buy us free
from our debt to the landlord.
We hadn't gotten far outside the city gate
when he raped me
and two other girls;
maybe it was part of his commission.
All brothels were on Fourth Street in 'the
  big world' of Shanghai.
I was supposed to keep one third of what I
  earned.

▲ *There are many female doctors and nurses in the People's Communes, and in the nursing centers of the factories.*

▲ *In farmers' homes, the older woman usually takes care of the cooking.*

▲ *"She won the first prize in riflery, in a competition which included all the boys."*

You often see women doing incredible balancing acts in the world-famous Chinese acrobatic performances.

But after they had deducted for rent and
   food
there was never anything left.
Even if I sometimes had twenty men a
   night,
if I refused somebody,
the manager of the brothel beat me bloody.
There were men from all nations,
but they all behaved alike.
Sometimes they cried on my shoulder
after they had slept with me.
and told me about someone they loved.
When the two years were up
they forced me to extend the contract.
My husband tried to get me out of it—
he walked all the way to Shanghai.
The police were paid off by the manager:
one free evening per week.
So my husband couldn't do anything.
He went home and hanged himself.
I know he loved me.
There were others—refined gentlemen—
who sold their wives to the brothel
after they had tired of them.
When the girls couldn't go on any longer
or when the customers didn't want them,
they were thrown out—I mean through the
   window
on the top floor.
It was called suicide.
The police turned the other way.
As I said, they had their free evening.
I was beautiful and strong
and managed to survive until the revolution came.
When we all helped to hang the manager of
   the brothel

I thought of my husband.
Now I'm remarried and happy.
My new husband knows about my past.
He says he loves me even more
because of the hard times I had—
and I believe him.
My first husband also loved me—
he who sold me to the Fourth Street."

When one hears about such a fate, as
described above in a home for rehabilita-
ting former prostitutes, one can better understand the Puritan morality of the new China.
The Chinese regard our modern sexual freedom as philistine. We live in a society where
even advertising for sewing machines or har-
vester combines has sexual overtones. Such
things are thought to be bourgeois decadence
by the Chinese. In their society, sex is de-
emphasized to the extent that the citizens
find it easier to live up to their rigid sexual
ethic. Even for the young and newly married,
work and patriotism come first.

"I am twenty-two years old and married
to a soldier in the People's Liberation Army.
My husband was called up for two years, and I
am staying with my mother-in-law on her
farm. I meet my husband only once a year. We
will not have children for many years. I won
first prize in riflery in competition with all the
boys in our People's Commune. I am also
going to do military training. I want to be in
the artillery."

Testimony like this sounds fanatical, but
it was more depressing to listen to the bar-girls
in Hong Kong and Bangkok, who still live in
the old male-dominated society with its view
of women as commodities.

The leader of the women in the shoe polish factory displays their wares. ▼

Prostitution, along with the abuse of opium, was abolished in China practically overnight. In other areas such as women's liberation progress has taken longer . . . despite the fact that it has been a nominal law on the books all along. Even though women were guaranteed the same political and human rights as men in the party program of 1949 and in the Constitution of The People's Republic of China, it is a long climb to equality in the professions and in all the millions of small farmers' homes where the man has always been the head of the family.

What the Chinese have achieved up to now is almost enough. Nowhere in Asia—perhaps in the whole world—have women more closely reached equality with men. The women dress like men, perform the same heavy manual work, carry weapons and become soldiers. You have to look long and hard to find a glimpse what we used to call "typically feminine" coquetry. I would hate to be a cosmetics salesman in China. In Peking, forty per cent of all scientific and technical personnel is female, and women comprise twenty-two per cent of the National People's Congress.

In the revised constitution of January 17, 1975, it is expressly stated that "women have the same rights as men in *all* fields." Women have free access to contraceptives, abortions and sterilization, at their own request.

The women of Asia, one third of humanity, have hardly been taken into account up to now. Treated more like cattle and household utensils, at their very best they were considered property and became either mistresses with long fingernails and bound feet, or toys for tired warriors, or breeders of sons.

They are now starting to demand their rights, and their voices may yet decide the fate of the world. Everywhere I went I have seen

▲ *"There were eleven of us when we started in 1959. Ignorant housewives, all of us. Only two of us could read . . . now we sell shoe polish to a large part of the socialist world."*

them rise and demand the return of their human dignity. From the Mongolian steppes in the north to the rice-deltas of Cambodia in the south, fromthe factories of Shanghai in the east to the kibbutzim of Israel in the west, the same demand is heard. I wonder which way of life they will choose.

It is most difficult for me to believe that they will try to imitate western women. What I am afraid of instead is that they may once more submit to men's values in other forms, and unwittingly swallow their nationalism and militarism. I have never seen so many marching women as here in Asia, not only Chinese women but also Cambodian Buddhist girls with their soft limbs and Israeli sabra girls burning with patriotism. They are all saying that they are marching for peace. I wish I could believe them.

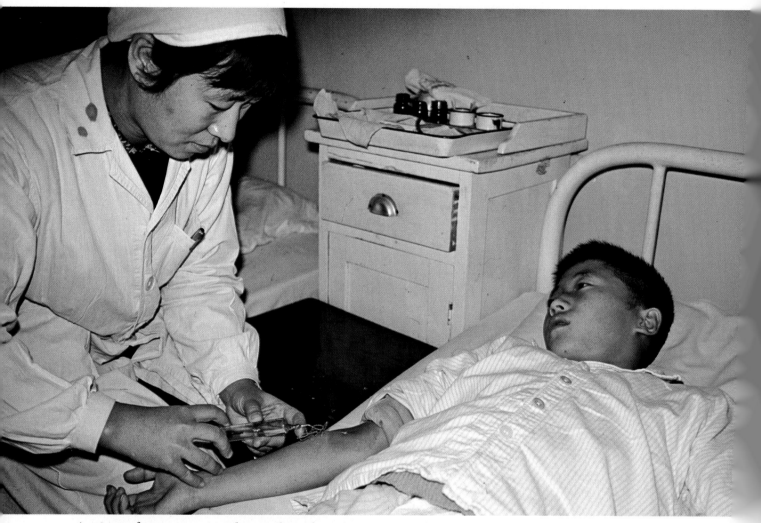

▲ *A modern nurse is educated in the traditional Chinese medicine as well as that of the western world.*

The young women of the countryside in a new and stimulating role, that of the sportswoman.

The story in another chapter of the female worker in the textile factory who was fired because she had smuggled her newborn son into the weaving mill is in no way unusual. At that time it was a catastrophe to become pregnant, for if it was discovered, the woman would be fired at once. Women often wrapped up their stomachs so tightly that their babies were deformed, or so weak that they died. A woman who had a baby did not have any other choice but to bring the child to the factory secretly to feed it. If the boss was near, the desperate mother might try to hide her little one under a machine. Sometimes a child lost its fingers in the machinery.

The most usual solution to this problem was for the grandparents to care for their grandchildren, a custom which is still widely practiced and which facilitates the enormous upward march of women in Chinese life, particularly the professions. This custom probably also contributes to the physical welfare of the elderly and is most unlike the barbaric western way of isolating aged people who may still be quite fit to work by casting them into idleness. Furthermore, there is an impressive number of day nurseries in towns and People's Communes for those who have no families to care for their children.

Suchou is famous for its silk mills and embroidery. Thirty per cent of industrial laborers in Suchou are women. 525 day nurseries care for more than 22,000 pre-school children. Women get three months off after childbirth, and the baby is then entitled to a place in a day nursery. Many of the parents leave children Monday through Saturday, a fact that gives rise to tourists' suspicion that Red China is opposed to family life and wishes to raise children like communist broiler chickens. That is really not true. The family institution is cherished by the Party. Couples are always seen affectionately dragging their small children along wherever they go and there is little divorce.

It cannot be denied that even very young children are exposed to strong ideological training, which has been itensified since the cultural revolution. Chinese children no longer read old fairy tales about dragons and giants. Instead, moralizing stories about proletarian heroes—like the helpful truck driver Lei Fung and the two courageous "sisters on the steppe"—are taught.

THE YOUNG AND THE OLD

◀ *I go to a day nursery in Shanghai, and I will soon be three years old.*

SCHOOLS IN CHINA

After the Revolution in 1949 Chinese teaching began to be patterned on Western ideas which were elitist in thought and therefore did not fit Mao's revolutionary message. Again, school problems were raised during the Cultural Revolution, and above all, the question "Who is school for?" was debated.

During the summer of 1966 I observed much change from "headmaster schools" to "people's schools," in which a few leaders were replaced by broadly-based committees. The principle now is to encourage school for everybody. Today, China has a need to educate between two and three hundred million people. And that is why questions concerning education are met with burning interest by all the public.

There has also been a strong effort to connect the schools more closely with the total society. They wish that large groups who are normally outside of the school system participate, rather than just observe it. This is what they call the "open door school," and a lot of workers, farmers, housewives, laborers and pensioners are taking part as so-called "amateur teachers."

There are many other interesting things to be observed in the new Chinese educational system, such as new systems of grading, practical versus theoretical work, physical and mental health, loyalty between companions and the responsibility of the teacher , to name a few.

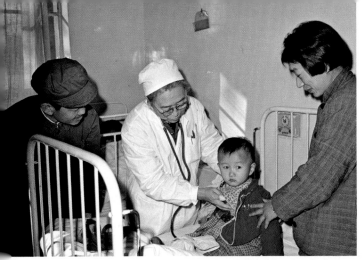

▲ *This day nursery in Peking has two pediatricians to check the health of the small children.*

▲ *Imagine the joy of dancing to the teacher's accordion music!*

▲ *We are being taught to help with the daily chores, so that we can do the same when we go home.*

▲ *Yu-Gi and her pals in Shanghai.*

▲ *A good soldier has to be fast at arithmetic.*

▲ *Chen Yen-yen and Lu Kuang-Ping will surely be good at English. Through studies in their own language, the children already have remakably well-trained memories, and a good ability to learn.*

Despite the fact that China is still an underdeveloped country, there are very few illiterates among the young people. At the most, ten per cent cannot read and they are mainly in the nomadic mountain and desert populations. About 135 million children are enrolled in the elementary schools, which cover between five and six years, and a further 35 million children are enrolled in middle schools.

The most important qualification for further study is the family's political zeal.

Chinese methods of education differ from ours in their training of children in "Mao Tsetung's thinking" and the communist ethic. It is reminiscent of the ethical-moral upbringing practiced by the Christian Church in the western world at the time when no other ideology was allowed. However, the Chinese

▲ *Swing merry-go-rounds are part of the playground equipment at this elementary school.*

▲ *It is nice to be able to be near grandmother when the stranger wants to take photographs.*

▲ *A dialogue, with the help of the schoolteacher, in a middle school in Nanking. Attention and order are noteworthly in Chinese classrooms.*

158

are much more effective than our clergymen and Sunday School teachers ever were. The result, as a French journalist wrote, is a nation of 800,000,000 Boy Scouts.

If you ask Chinese children in the huge center for play and education in Shanghai called the Children's Palace about their dreams and plans for the future, you will be answered according to the catechism. No one thinks of his own career or of earning money. They all want to serve the people and do whatever job the Party assigns to them. One wants to be a farmer, another a soldier in the Red Army, another a miner. No one wants to be an executive or a movie star.

Some sceptical westerners believe this is too good to be true. By all indications I have seen it *is* true. These really are the children's

▲ *The two-stringed violin is China's principal instrument, not only in the Peking opera, but in the school orchestra.*

▲ *Middle school pupils do practical farm work one month of every school year. They are also taught to operate motorized equipment.*

▲ *Morning exercises for 2,000 pupils at a middle school in Peking.*

159

dreams of the future. Is that good, or do my doubts originate from the incurable mark of my own culture's individualism? For the small Chinese in the Children's Palace, there is no longer any choice between good and evil.

On the other hand, much is valuable in the Chinese educational system which I accept without reservation and would like to import to the west. There are no material rewards for the children. Financial scholarships are thought to nurture materialism. A diligent and conscientious pupil can be elected the "pupil of the five virtues."

▲ *Millions of students from high schools and universities help to plant and to harvest rice.*

▲ *Ni Chi-chin, unofficial world high jump champion in 1970. He now works as a teacher of young people interested in sports.*

▲ *The wall newspapers at the teachers' school in Nanking in Spring, 1976 say "Like master, like man! We don't like the way the university teaches. The criticism was directed against the man who was the Minister of Education. As a result of the students' action, he was forced to leave.*

▲ *University students experiment with modern data-processing equipment.*

▲ *Pupils in a high school in Nanking study the effect of chemicals on different plants.*

▲ *Elementary school pupils produce bottle brushes in the school's own factory.*

▲ *"We are singing about working in the cotton factory." Even in nursery school, Chinese children take field trips to study different ways of working.*

▲ *A unique form of education takes place in the "officials" schools. These are boarding schools, situated in the country, with the theme of "learning from farmers." Through association with farmers and workers, the government hopes to keep down the number of arrogant and autocratic bureaucrats.*

▲ *Transport workers from Shanghai are thinning out lettuce in their garden plot.*

162

Sending youths as well as older white-collar workers out from the cities to do hard labor among the poor farming peasants is another excellent institution in China. "This is our new University," many Chinese say. A group of about thirty youths is sent out at least once a year for an extended period. From a modest beginning, this system has grown to involve tens of millions of young people every year not for a summer holiday, but for hard, dirty work.

There is opposition to the system in many quarters, especially among the city teen-agers, who may be sent out to the country at the completion of their schooling, possibly never to return.

Carrying manure to fertilize land high on the mountainsides is said to be especially beneficial. It probably is, for the most impor-

▲ *In China, old people usually remain at home with their relatives. These old ones live in a nursing home in Tientsin for those who have no relatives. Three doctors and twelve nurses offer preventive health services. "Early discovery, and early cure" is the rule.*

tant aim of this project is neither to give city children country air nor to give farmers cheap labor. It is the equalization of classes—to create understanding and appreciation among the students and privileged city-dwellers of the hundreds of millions of anonymous and hardworking farmers, who still carry China on their shoulders despite industrialization. It is valuable for one who is studying medicine to have learned the farmers' and workers' milieu and to have experienced their conditions and occupational diseases. This is but

163

▲ *In the hobby room there are TV, chess and all kinds of literature; here they also organize studies and exercise.*

This is the tale of the old dockworker, Lee Feng-tai:

"In my family there were four of us, father, mother, my sister and I. Father worked in the docks from early to late, but there was never enough money, not even for food. Until I was eight years old I had never tasted rice; we lived on cabbage leaves. When I was 18, I followed my father to the docks, and in spite of the fact that we were both working, we couldn't earn enough to support ourselves. My sister was sold by the age of fourteen.

"Once, I fell while carrying a heavy sack. A superior saw that the sack had burst and beat me to unconciousness. I laid ill for three days without any food, but my working companions helped me back to health. My father got asthma and so did my mother. Father died on August 15, 1945, and I didn't have a penny. Comrades at the docks collected money for the funeral.

"Though there was only my mother and me left, we couldn't get enough to eat, not on my salary. One day my mother called for me; she was dying of asthma. She wanted me to go and get more food from my working place. When I returned the next day, my mother was dead. My fellow workers helped me again. I couldn't stay in my old home, because the landlady said that, as I didn't have enough money, I had better live at the docks. A sack of straw and a jacket saved my life that winter. In 1949 the whole country was liberated by our great leader, Mao. Today we live a happy life, but before, in the old society, we suffered all the time. We had to live like horses and oxen, and eat like cats and dogs. In the socialist home for aged people, my comrades have shown me great care and attention. It is here I want to end my days."

▲ *Six o'clock on a winter morning in a park in Tientsin. Vigorous pensioners carrying their wooden swords are just about to start training in wushu.*

◄ *A healthy eighty-six-year-old man in Shanghai.*

A doctor of acupuncture must know almost 400 pressure points, divided into fourteen "meridians." Training models are filled with water and coated with paint. If you hit the right point, some liquid oozes out. ▶

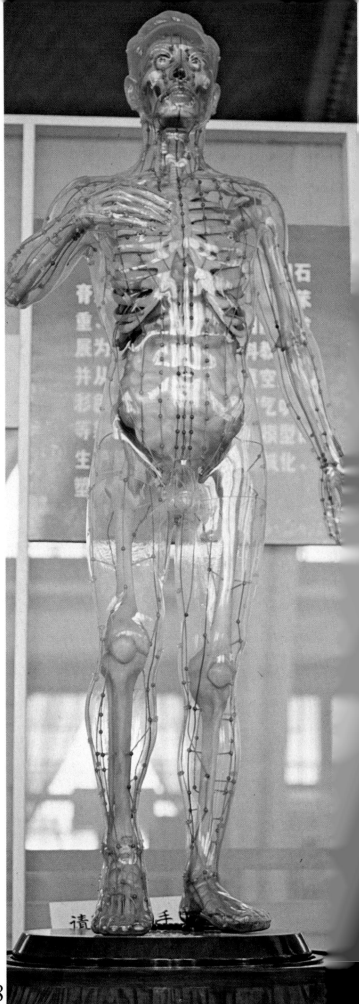

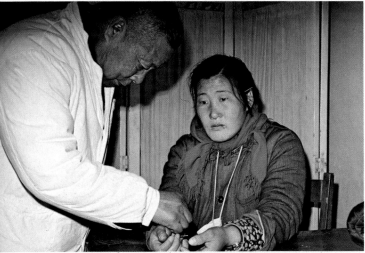

▲ A doctor of acupuncture treating his patient for an infection, with needles at the temple and the wrist.

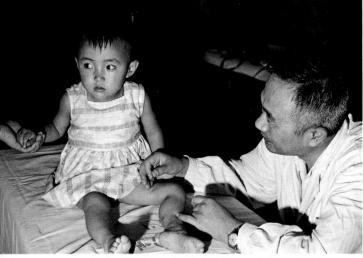

▲ When I showed movies of this doctor and his patient on television, almost fifteen years ago, an associate professor in medicine telephoned me to complain about this "humbug."

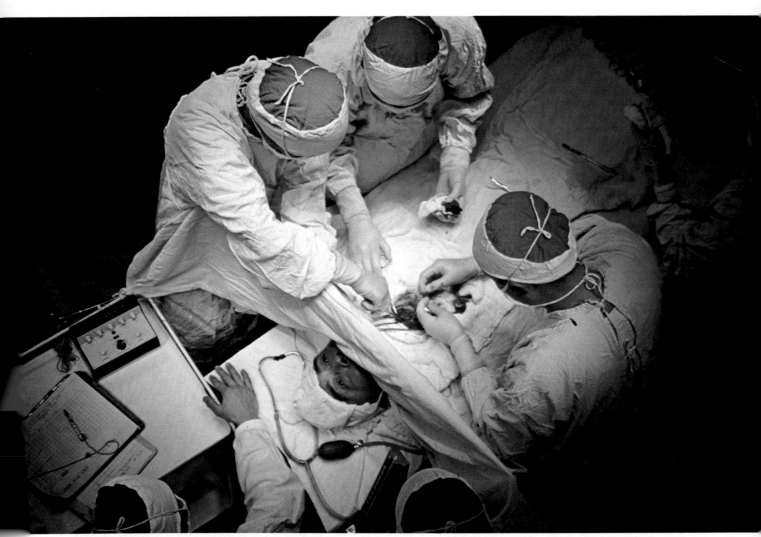

▲ *In January, 1976, I witnessed this operation to remove a tumor of the throat. The patient had chosen to be anesthetized solely by acupuncture needles. The operation lasted two hours, and he was fully awake all the time, communicating with the nurse controlling the electric impulsator connected to the needles. This hospital had performed 4,500 successful operations with acupuncture. We now know that about ten per cent of people are immune to this kind of anesthetic. Today acupuncture technique is the subject of research and serious interest outside of China.*

Chinese doctors making their rounds. ▼

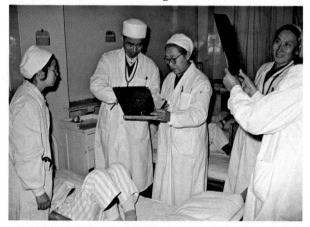

one example. In order to enter a high school or university, a student must participate in hard manual labor for at least two years. There are few exceptions.

Almost every old man or woman I spoke to in China praised the Red regime, and told horrifying stories of how old people had lived before the Revolution. In the beginning I was somewhat skeptical. I had read Marco Polo, who wrote that the Chinese had a form of primitive social care in the thirteenth century. And the Portuguese, Mendes Pintos, was so impressed by the "heathen" Chinese welfare organizations in the sixteenth century that his book was censored by the Inquisition. But gradually I realized that what the old people were telling me was not propaganda cliches. Testimonies from travellers and missionaries during the last two centuries confirm it. Ac-

▲ *A "barefoot doctor" with her well-filled doctor's bag and ready smile.*

170

tually the highly-touted respect for the old was mainly an excuse for hidebound government by greybeards, and did not prevent the elderly poor from starving to death in the streets. It is not very difficult to imagine the plight of lonely old people around the turn of the century when we know that there were more than five million beggars in the provinces of Kiangsu and Anhwei alone.

The communists have not only conquered starvation, they have also instituted good care for old people. Old men and women without relatives had previously been reduced to begging. These people now live in homes for the aged, which do not meet our standards, but are well-tended and humane all the same. Industrial workers receive a pension of seventy per cent of their former salaries. Men are pensioned at the age of sixty, women at fifty. The physical vigor of the Chinese is surprising. You seldom see soft, overly-fat bodies. This is partly because the Chinese still live so near subsistence level that they seldom get the ailments of rich and luxurious living, and partly because of the importance the communists have always placed on physical fitness. Typically, Chairman Mao was a well-known swimming enthusiast himself.

▲ *A new method of vaccination powered by compressed air being demonstrated at a medical equipment trade show.*

171

SPORTS IN CHINA

To us, sports are physical training and competition. In China they talk about "physical culture," a broader outlook. According to the old philosophy, the Chinese look upon body and soul as a unified whole, which is reflected in that form of traditional physical culture known as *wushu.*

Sport activities are directed nationally by a central organization, the All Chinese Sports Federation, which divides the country into provinces, districts and trades. Economic profit in connection with sports is forbidden. The Chinese also frown upon intense competiton.

The international sports world has been confused by the Chinese because of their theory of "friendship first, competition second." Behind this philosophy lies the feeling that sports enables people to get on familiar terms with each other, internationally as well as at home.

In front of the entrance to the oldest high school for physical education in the country, outside Peking, is a magnificient statue of Chairman Mao. The motto of headmaster Cheng and his associates is a slogan from one of Mao's writings which can be read in the background: "Develop physical culture for the people's health." ▼

▲ *The school has a capacity of 2,000 pupils and good facilities for sports on which China wishes to concentrate.*

▲ *They take great interest in swimming, and the pool is of Olympic size.*

▲ *Next to ping-pong, the national sport, oddly enough, is basketball. This school has twenty-six courts.*

▲ *Groups from factories and workshops attend the high school, as well as students of education.*
These girls are going to be coaches.

◄ *Millions of young people train in the evenings, in the so-called "leisure schools."*

▲ *Gynmastics seems to be well-suited to the agile and supple Chinese. Many of the country's best teachers and instructors participate.*

175

▲ *I met these champions in a factory yard in Wuhan. This is the ancient form of wrestling, where it is permissible to throw your opponent on the hard ground.*

The old art of *wushu* is a combination of gymnastics, shadow-boxing and meditation exercises similar to yoga. Everywhere in the parks of Peking and Nanking old men and women can be seen practicing this slow, ritual dance.

Wherever you see Chinese participants in sport or gymnastics, you cannot help but be impressed with their seriousness and attention to training. Note the intensity of concentration on the faces of the people in these pictures and you'll immediately appreciate that physical development and discipline override the pleasure of winning.

▲ *Girls especially have made world records in archery.*

▲ *Starting-block training. Tibet has the outside track.*

Violent jumps and turns are part of wushu, which requires great physical fitness and speed. ▶

At six o'clock the new shift starts at Peking's Cotton Factory No. 3. But first, a fifteen-minute warm-up before work. ▼

▲ *In Peking's new Sports Hall, international table-tennis teams compete before an audience of 18,000. The floor can be rolled back to expose an artificial ice-hockey rink.*

180

▲ *Another sport is Tai-Chi-Chuan, which we sometimes simply call "shadow-boxing." It is a series of totally relaxed movements of 175 elements, all performed in a slow, gliding and circling style. This series of pictures shows four typical positions.*

He was a textile worker, but in his spare time he wrote short stories and novels. In Sweden, he would have been called a proletarian author. Tang Ke-hsin could not even write his own language well when his work was first published. He had gone to school for only three years, and his parents were illiterate. He had worked in a factory since he was ten years old. When he sent his first short story to a literary magazine, he couldn't write one fourth of the eight hundred words that he needed. He was forced to leave gaps or invent his own characters.

YOU ARE OUR VOICE

After a week of nervous waiting—all authors feel the same—he received a thick envelope from the magazine. Quite depressed, he let it lie there all day before he could bring himself to open it. It was his short story being returned—but it had been accepted. The editor had sent it back corrected, so that Tang Ke-hsin could learn the missing characters.

Thanks to the magazine and helpful fellow-workers, Tang could start studying at night school to learn to write his own language properly. Gradually he wrote more and bigger stories. They all told of the hard lives of factory workers among dye vats and bobbins.

"Spring Has Come to the Factory" was no love story, but the tale of a new air-conditioner for a department previously known as "the stinking hell." The author's own mother had sacrificed her life there. Old workers in the factory who had suffered for years in the hot dye-works wept for joy when the story was read to them.

"We have always been mute," the workers said. "Now you are our voice." Tang Ke-hsin's great difficulty as compared to ours was the Chinese written language. In our writing, we use one character for each sound. The Chinese use one character for each word. In order to be able to read and write simple prose, you must master several thousand signs. To be able to write their classic literature, you must master many times this number. Far into our century, the Chinese had no other way of writing. Only recently have they begun to simplify their written language.

The advantage of the Chinese system is that all regions of China can understand the common written language even though their spoken words can differ as much as Swedish and Italian. In spite of the different dialects, the written characters are the same. The dis-

▲ 110 *seamstresses worked with the finest silk for a year on this colossal embroidery (about 9½ feet high by 26 feet wide).*

advantages, however, far outweigh the advantages. Imagine what a Chinese typewriter looks like. In the old Chinese society, writing separated the classes, and was an insurmountable barrier for those who wanted to take the step from uneducated to educated.

Not until well into our century did the system become more democratic. In 1917, the year of the Russian Revolution, when so much that was old and decadent collapsed, the bell tolled also for the ancient Chinese written language. The poet and philologist He Shih called for a more democratic language, which he called Pai-hua. This happened at about the same time that the students of Peking started demonstrating against foreign imperialists who had oppressed China for nearly a hundred years.

Hu Shih's reform was a necessary condition of the revolution and made possible the entire new literature of China. Without it, writers like Tang Ke-hsin would have been voices without vocal cords.

The first generation authors who wrote in Pai-hua, with very few exceptions, were not especially politically conscious. They were all middle class, and their most important task was to teach themselves and others to use the new written language. It was a laborious process, like a stumbling old Chinese woman whose feet had been bound trying to learn to walk.

▲ *Here the leader of the difficult and necessary work in the oil fields of Taching is being immortalized in a student painting.*

▲ *Typing in China means being able to choose quickly among 3,000 different characters!*

Textile worker Tang Ke-hsin from Shanghai, who wrote about how "Spring Comes to the Factory." ▶

186

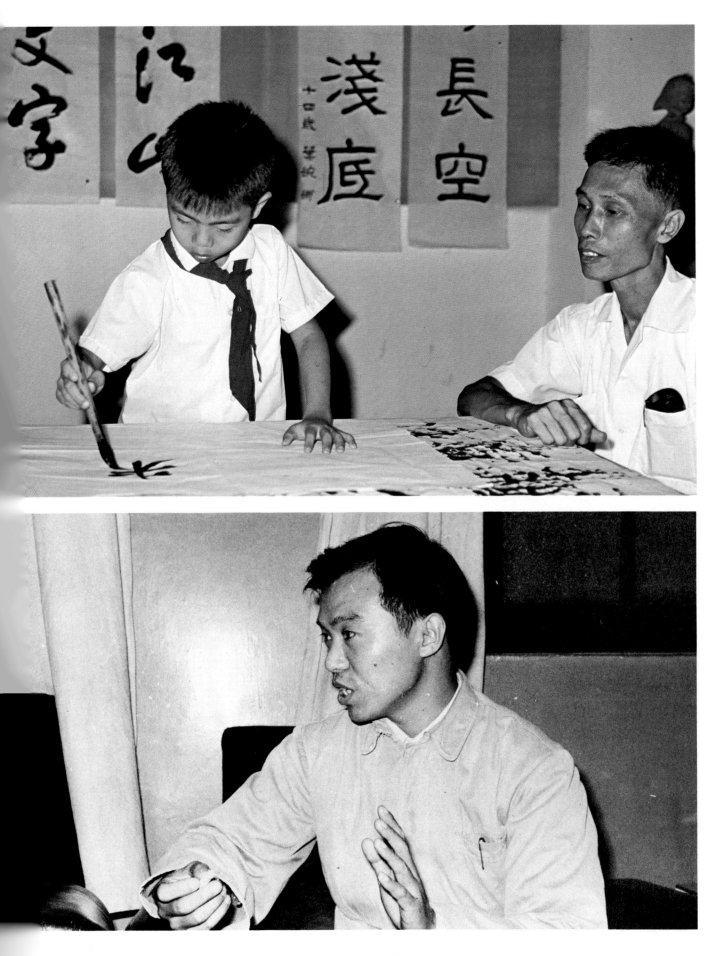

Illustration for Lu Hsün's famous short story, "The True Story of Ah Q." It deals with a decadent opportunist of ancient China who was an admirer of all things western. ▶

Gradually, literature grew beyond the traditional. Chinese lyric poetry was customarily philosophical poetry about nature, with abundant quantities of birds and moonshine, snow and flowers. Now it more often interprets the new national feeling among the Chinese. Wen I-tos' famous poem "The Laundry" was written while he was in exile in America:

"To wash is a dirty job,
only fit for Chinese, you tell me.
But did I not hear one of your preachers say
that Christ was an ordinary carpenter?
Do you believe that? Do you really believe
    that?

What can you do with soft soap and water?
What is that against building warships?
It is not much of a future for you
to wash the sweat of others with your own
    sweat.
Do you want that? Do you really want
    that?"

The majority of the Chinese revolution's great prose writers made their début about 1920. The most important was Lu Hsün. His satire was not so much against the cruel bullies in the old society as against the passive victims who did not have the courage to strike back, much less consider a revolution. Lu Hsün himself became a communist after the Shanghai massacres.

In 1930, the association of "Left Radical Authors" was founded. It had clearly framed political aims which were close to communism. Earlier Chinese literature had dealt with princes, warriors, landowners, mandarins, courtesans. Now authors like Tang Kehsin wanted to give expression to those who had been voiceless: the poor and the unpropertied.

Mao Tun's *Silkworms in Spring* deals with the small landowners who fell more and more in debt the harder they toiled. Lao She's *A Ricksha in Peking* is about the big city's proletariat. The hero of this big, harrowing novel is called Happy Boy. The woman he falls

188

in love with is called Little Lucky Girl. The names are ironic seen against the background of their bearers' destinies. Most appalling is the misery of Happy Boy as he destroys not only his body but also his morals. The description is so merciless that western translators have added a happy ending, where the hero at last wins the girl. In the orginal version, he hangs himself.

Poetry also lets the poor speak. A common theme is the stench from the old rotten society. Tsang Ko-chia uses it in his famous poem "The Zero of Life." It was inspired by a small notice in a Shanghai paper about 800 children drowned by a tidal wave:

"Let the fashionable ladies step on you with a yell.
Let those bodies bleed and rot
and let the stench mingle
with the breath of the big Shanghai."

Most of Mao Tse-tung's own poems were

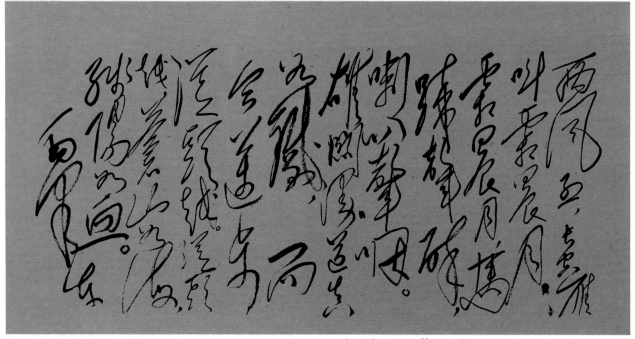

▲ *Mao's calligraphy*

189

written in the beginning of the 1930s, "hummed forth on horseback," as the poet himself has said.

The strange thing about them is that they are written in the old style in spite of their revolutionary content. When writing about the Long March, Mao takes his style from the poets who lived about one thousand years ago in the Sung period:

"The Red Army does not fear the pains of the Long March.
One thousand mountains and ten thousand rivers are nothing compared to it.
The mountains with five peaks are to it no higher than waves.
Wumeng's huge chains roll by like balls of clay.
Warm are the Golden Sand River's foam-washed cliffs.
Cold are the iron links over the big Tatu River.
Heavy snowclouds over Minshan are their happiness.
When at last we are there, everybody's face is smiling."

During the war against the Japanese and the civil war, poetry and theatre in the Red provinces were encouraged at the expense of prose because the rural public there was less able to read than the urban populations. Workers and farmers could only be reached by the spoken word, and lyric poetry was an oral art often recited or sung.

A master painting motifs on a small snuff bottle. ▶

190

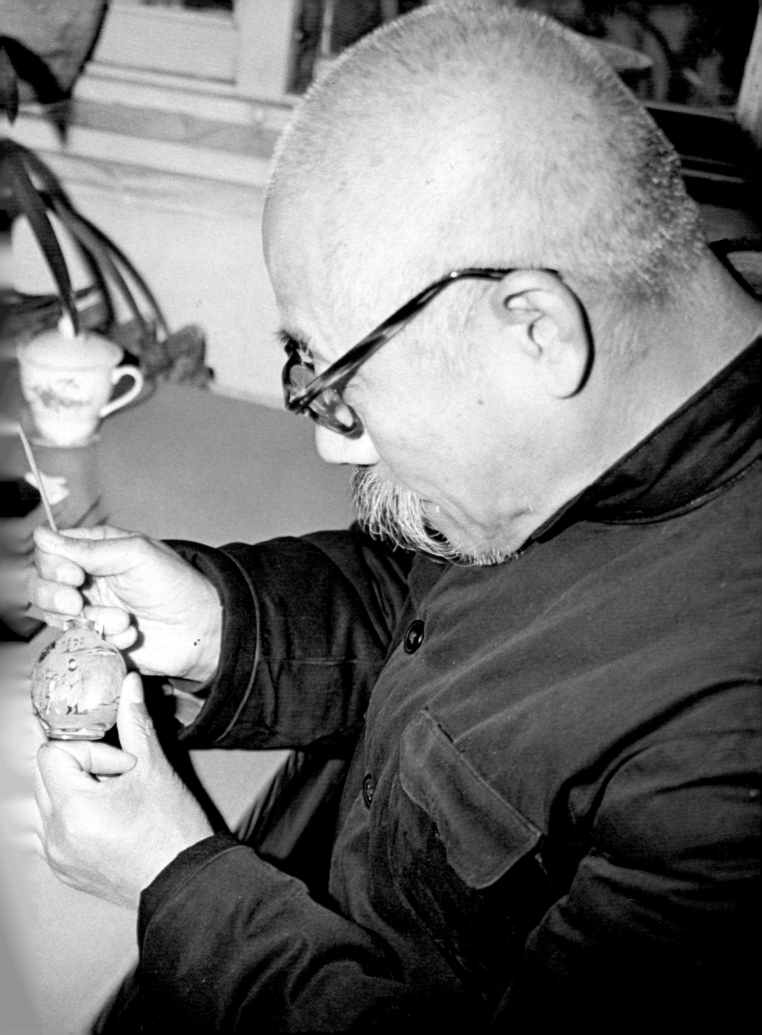

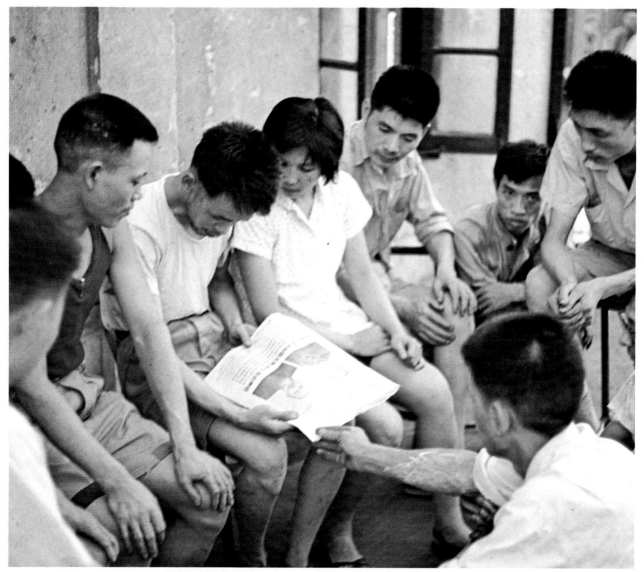

▲ *"You are our voice." Workers in a bicycle factory gather around a fellow worker who can read. The newspaper says that Mao has announced that China will support North Vietnam.*

▲ *Ivory has been carved by hand for thousands of years. In a modern workshop, artists carve with the help of electrical tools.*

▲ *A traditional Peking handicraft is cloissonné. Here color is being applied in the patterns of metallic arabesques.*

▲ *A showpiece.*

During the Cultural Revolution, Chinese society was shaken. Even the children were involved, sometimes in a way which must seem offensive to us. ▶

On the other hand, drama was the genre most often used in the political battle. The Red Army and the communists were often unknown, terrifying conceptions for people in remote districts. There the theatre, with its power for direct agitation, was effective. The actors were often soldiers. They played in village market places and factories, with utterly primitive staging.

Old Chinese opera, often called Peking opera, was a popular form of art, at which the connoisseurs turned up their noses. The actors were always men, even in women's parts. The singing was forced, the voices high and falsetto, unendurable to our ears. The actors not only mastered singing and acting; opera also required elements of acrobatics. It is a wonderful experience to see a Chinese opera star suddenly start juggling with five swords and turning somersaults over the heroine's bed.

After the Revolution, the old popular opera form was retained, but given new and revolutionary content. In the new operas, the fights against the Japanese and Chiang Kai-shek are described. "The Red Torch" is about a railway worker who organizes the resistance of the oppressed, and finally dies a martyr in prison. In "The White-Haired Girl," Red partisans receive assistance from a recluse girl who lives in the mountains.

Opera and drama remain popular by reproducing experiences shared by the public.

"We met a girl just like this when fighting against the Japanese up in the mountains," one of my Chinese hosts said when we saw "The White-Haired Girl" in the opera house in Shanghai.

In recent years art and literature in China have become increasingly political and orthodox. Their moralism and constant preaching are reminiscent of our old Christian religious literature. The progress which has been made is more quantitative than qualitative. Collections of poems appear in huge numbers, and poetry clubs are being formed by the tens of thousands. One feels that this is done not by orders from above, but as an expression of spontaneous enthusiasm. Every achievement in farming, every new power plant or bridge gives birth to a new tidal wave of poetry. One special genre is poetry complimentary to Mao Tse-tung, which uses traditional symbols formerly reserved for the emperor or the gods.

194

No other mortals could be compared to the sun and the stars.

"Chairman Mao
you are the sun that never sets.
You shine like the Great Bear.
We miners will always follow you.
With the morning sun in our hearts
we will faithfully serve the Revolution,
exterminate the wolves and raise the red
  banner,
and write a new page
in the book of history."

All these unknown people's poets are like amateur authors who tell simple stories with a strong moral coloration.

In 1966 the Cultural Revolution broke out. Since then, Chinese literature has become, if possible, still more political. Earlier, they had tried to obtain so-called social realism, with somewhat restrained character description, and complex problems. Now the Chinese catchwords are revolutionary realism and revolutionary romance. This means that national inheritance is given greater importance, and that authors may write only about proletarian heroes or class enemies as black as night.

The ancient Peking opera is now prohibited. In October, 1965, I saw the classic opera, "The Female Generals," in Peking. When I returned the next year, there was no longer any possibility of enjoying this sort of opera, with its feudal upper class heroes.

The decline in artistic quality after the Revolution, both in the Soviet Union and in China, is believed by some to be partially due to the lack of freedom and to a more rugged spiritual climate. That is one side of the truth, but there is also another—the effect of the lack of villains on literature. Formerly inspired by hatred of those in power, now suddenly the authors are on the victors' side. Poetry no longer tears down, but rebuilds—no longer depicts the negative with hatred and disgust, but praises the positive, which is always less rewarding. Thus post-Revolutionary literature often becomes edifying in the dreariest sense of the word.

"You are our voice," the old workers said to Tang Ke-hsin. To be the voice of the oppressed, here, as in China, is the aim and meaning of literature. In spite of everything, during the past fifty years Chinese literature has lived up to this motto. As never before, it has become the voice of the people. It would be tragic if it were to become so propagandistic and so moralistic that it would no longer be worthy of the name of literature. In that case, it would be opposed to the directives which Mao Tse-tung gave in his famous lectures in the Yenan base "About Literature and Art." He said that literature and art have, as their first duty, to serve the people and promote the Revolution. But he also said, with great emphasis, that "pieces of art without artistic quality have no power, however progressive they may be politically."

One motto was "Take a firm grip on the revolution and raise production." Criticism against bosses and foremen was written in large characters and displayed, as in this picture. ▶

I wrote this for a Swedish newspaper to accompany my pictures of what may have been the largest mass meeting of the Cultural Revolution, on a late summer day in Shanghai, 1966:

"I am awakened in the early morning by the sounds of the street, but the noises are not the usual rattling of cars, buses and millions of bicycles. The noise comes from the crowds of people who, with shuffling feet in their rubber soled shoes, are streaming along the streets. Silent and determined, with rolled-up banners and flags, they are marching to one place; the big parade ground and marketplace of Shanghai.

"Today the rally is for Vietnam. One million Chinese wish to show Ho Chi Minh and his embattled people their sympathy. With meticulous precision, group after group forms in order in front of the enormous red placards above the platform. Speaker follows speaker. The crowd answers. The tempo rises. Finally a general, a representative of the Chinese Army, appears. His words make the vast crowd roar.

"The voices roll like thunder bouncing from house to house. 'The Chinese people are like a living ocean, whose waves will help the Vietnamese people wash the imperialist attackers into the sea. . . .Shoulder to shoulder we stand and we are strongly determined to support our fighting brothers . . .'

"Like a trumpet blast comes the answer from the crowd. In unison, one million people shout a cry. Fast, short, high, with the penetrating Chinese voice—it is like a colossal wave of sound which rises over the human throng. They start in unison, and stop just as sharply.

"An hour later the main speaker is a North Vietnamese general. A murmur of expectation arises from the crowd, as they perceptibly shift their feet. Suddenly everything is strangely silent. The human picture changes its dimensions, its intensity grows with the stillness and at last I understand.

" 'Once more we shall win.' General Vo Nguyen Giap, commander of the Vietnamese People's Army, blasts forth this slogan. I catch a glimpse of the lone speaker, like a dot high up on the platform. The loudspeakers shout out his message about a sister nation who has been attacked. The general speaks calmly and distinctly. Every now and then he is echoed by the crowd, and the echo has an enormous effect, an echo so strong that I wish that the whole world was able to hear it."

▲ *Millions of people under flags are marching and singing out on the legendary Nanking Road.*

198

▲ *Students with clenched fists demonstrating to show their solidarity.*

▲ *During the Cultural Revolution, I often saw people in buses and public places reading aloud from Chairman Mao's "Little Red Book."*

Lu-Shan is a beautiful mountain area, often celebrated in song. The largest fresh-water lake in China, Poyang Hu, is situated in these mountains.
▶

▲ In the Workers' Museum in Tientsin, one can see exhibits about the history of our time. This man lost one of his eyes when, as a young man, he worked in one of the imperialist workshops with no safety equipment.

▲ In the '40s, wretched workers held secret meetings at night to plan to sabotage production in the workshops and factories, often owned by Japanese or westerners.

▲ *Some unsafe machines were used without the slightest consideration for the workers.*

▲ *A leader in the Workers' Commune in Tientsin, was forced to work at pulling a ricksha. His fingers were cut off by a machine and he could find no other work.*

▲ *Here he tells the youth of today how ruthlessly workers used to be exploited.*

▲ *The old Peking opera, and its world of make-believe, have been replaced by stories from the everyday life during the Revolution. This exhibit represents a famous scene from one of them.*

Corn for an undeveloped country in Africa is loaded in the harbor. During the night a deceitful foreman slips some sacks away...

▲ *A popular dockworker has been enticed into the plot by the love of adventure. An older fellow worker brings him to his senses.*

▲ *The plot is uncovered by a female party secretary and others. The persons involved are censured, and must replace the stolen goods.*

▲ *A popular theme of some revolutionary opera is honesty. In this scene, grain to be shipped to an under-developed country in Africa is taken on board. A dishonest foreman lets some sacks disappear during the night.*

▲ *At the end, the actors honor the audience by singing the "Internationale."*

Heavily loaded junks sail the mud laden water of the Yang-tze River.

▲ *Revolutionary opera is written simply so that it can be understood by the uneducated masses.*

▲ *On one of my earlier trips I found that several of the classic Peking operas were still being produced. For example, "The White Snake"—a tale of two snakes, one white and one blue. The gods transform them into two beautiful human beings, the girl Pai Su-chen, and her lady's maid, Ching Erh. Pai has a wonderful love affair, but the jealous monk, Fa Hai, tries his best to spoil it. Happily, the story ends well for all.*

▲ A picture of Mei Lan-fang, a legendary actor of the old school. In most operas men performed male and female roles.

▲ In old operas, dance often was the means of bringing romance and realism together.

Operatic music is played on percussion, string, and wind instruments. The moon-guitar (yuchchien) and the Peking violin (chinghu) are the most important, and give the music its distinctive tone. ▶

▲ "Heroic Sacrifice" is the name of this opera about a young officer during the Sung Dynasty who sacrifices his life for his native country.

▲ In spite of all, Peking opera is sometimes very realistic. In order to play realistic battles, actors are trained in acrobatics and in the handling of arms.

▲ *A new and popular art is folk painting. This picture is called "Who Has Cleaned in Front of My Door?"*

◄ *A decorative screen with heroic themes from the history of China. The inlays in the wooden surface are metal, mother-of-pearl, soapstone or jade.*

▲ *A combination of lines and rich colors.*

▲ *On their way to the village.*

An artistic work in ivory honoring the Revolution. ▼

THE DREAM OF MAN

To the Chinese, life on earth has always been more important than the after-life. They have been more understanding of those religions which aim at improving the conditions of life on earth, and producing decent human beings. They say maybe the supernatural does exist,

As always in China, mother love is very
strong.

▲ *"Teach one another" is a common theme in all work.*

▲ *From gasoline drum into wood stove—a good example of recycling.*

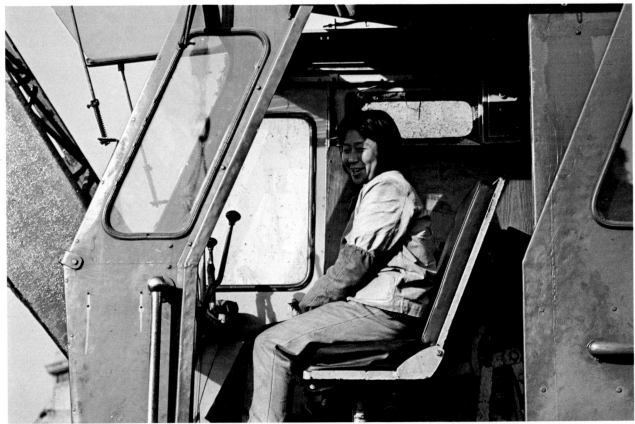

▲ *Women have equal rights in all jobs. This woman is a crane operator.*

The glorious peaks of the mountains of Tibet.

▲ *The newest models of Chinese tractors can easily make their way through the flooded rice-fields.*

▲ *Without water there is no harvest. Everyone is happy with the new irrigation system.*

▲ *Two nice girls in the arms of the Laughing Buddha in Hangchou. The younger generation regards this religious figure as a fairy-tale character.*

▲ *The sluggish giant panda, with its sometimes manlike behavior, is everybody's favorite.*

▲ *They use their paws as hands, peeling sugar cane and bamboo with ease. Their solemn look charms many of the visitors.*

A great leader has departed this life.
Chou-En-lai and his memory are honored by
millions of Peking's citizens at the hero's
monument at Tien-An-Men square. ▶

With tear-filled eyes and clenched fists, these
schoolgirls quote the deceased Chou and
promise to carry on his work and the
Revolution. ▼

◄ *Chou En-lai.*

Large groups and single citizens march and carry paper wreaths with the monogram of the deceased. ▼

including a Heaven, a Creator, and good and evil spirits, but if they do, they should be worshipped with beautiful ceremonies and from a respectful distance. How we behave toward our fellow men and how the state and the society function are far more important to the Chinese.

Religion has never been as important in China as it has been in the west. Innumerable temples were built, and some of them still exist, but as soon as religion threatened the power of the emperor, he crushed it. Otherwise, religions were left alone. When the Chinese Communists forbade religious proselytizing in the country, saying that religion must remain a private matter, they were following another one of their old traditions. Further, religion has never played the important and influential role it does for example, in India, or the Arab world, or in the west. Strict moral rules, bans on wine or on certain foods, wrestling against sin and guilt, fanatic interest in salvation, persecution of people holding a different opinion, were all unknown in China.

For two thousand years the dominant philosophy of the ruling classes was Confucianism. Its founder was "The Wise King" (in Chinese, K'ung Fu-tzu or in Latin, Confucius). He lived in the sixth century B.C. and therefore was a contemporary of the Buddha,

▲ A woodcut of Confucius (K'ung Fu-tzu). The Wise King of ancient China was the great philisopher. Today he is often regarded as a dangerous reactionary.

the first Greek philosophers and the first Jewish prophets. Like Jesus and Socrates, Confucius wrote nothing himself but his words were gathered by disciples into a book *The Lun Yu* or *The Talks*. His brief words of wisdom were studied by all educated Chinese, and pre-Revolutionary officials were tested on their knowledge of them. Confucianism is more a moral doctrine than a religion. As such, it was immensely influential in the life and customs of ancient China. In many ways *The Talks* advocated high moral values. Many of Confucius' words are similar to Jesus' teaching. For example, Confucius said, "what I do not want the people to do to me, neither shall I do to them."

Today, Confucius' writings are reproached for their conservatism. He shows too much respect for everything that is old. He bows deeply to the emperor, and indeed to all authorities. His teachings became a weapon in the hands of the rulers, and an obstacle to necessary changes of the Revolution.

While Confucianism is being cast aside today as upper-class learning, the other prominent domestic religion, Taoism, is being condemned as superstitious. The holy writings of Taoism are called *Tao Te King* and are said to have been written by Lao-tzu, who also lived in the sixth century B.C. Legend tells us that Lao-tzu was born with white hair, and that among other things he spoke to a plum tree at birth. Some modern researchers doubt his actual existence.

Tao means "the way." Tao is the power which embraces all and which governs everything—not by power or violence, but merely by exisiting as the beginning and the end of the universe, like water or dust, the humble elements to which everything returns. Tao is the deepest felt and the highest aspiration in life, much as God is to Christians, but a god which has no person, cannot be described, and has no form or definitive characteristics.

With time, Taoism came to be regarded more and more as a supersitition. The Taoists tried to contact the Tao by short cuts with magic and amulets and all sorts of hocus-pocus rather than through the original medium of meditation. The Tao priests were no longer the holy men of old and, instead, regarded as charlatans.

In Communist China, the Taoists have tried to adjust their old beliefs of forsaking the world and have tried to re-interpret them in a socialist manner. "The world" and "earthly property" are now construed to mean "private property," but this change notwithstanding, the teachings are declining in popularity.

One of the most beloved divinities in China is Kwan-yin, the goddess of mercy. She is present in thousands of temples and millions of homes, though often dusty and forgotten. Those who were threatened by poverty and disease, by robbers and unjust officials, would pray to her. She has also been called "Our Mother, who gives us children," and could almost be described as a Chinese Virgin Mary.

Kwan-yin came from India to China with Buddhism. Buddhism became the religion for the great masses, to which Confucianism gave neither "strength for the struggle of life, nor comfort in the hour of death." The Chinese chose the milder and more tolerant branch of Buddhism called "The Great Wagon." There

View of the great plains of central China, in Kiangsi province. The yellow waters of the Yang-tze River can be seen faintly on the horizon.

▲ *A row of inscrutable gilded Buddhas in a temple in Huhehot.*

are still about one hundred million Buddhists in China, but their number is rapidly being reduced.

In Red China, Buddhism has the same freedom and the same restrictions as other religions. It may be practiced but not propagated. Many of the monasteries have been taken over by the state and are treated as ancient monuments. In Tibet and Inner Mongolia, there is a special form of Buddhism, called Lamaism. Its leader is the Dalai Lama. When he dies, the country is canvassed for a newborn babe in whom the Dalai Lama it is believed will be reborn. It may take several years before the right babe is found.

I was allowed to visit one of the city's Lama temples in Huhehot, the capital of Inner Mongolia. There were twenty-six monks, all very old, except for "The Living Buddha", who was 27 years old. He sat on a sort of throne while the others prayed. The temple was seven hundred years old, older than the city, and in the dusk I could catch a glimpse of iridescent prayer-strips and innumerable statues of the Buddha. The whole impression was that of a scene unconnected with the present. My Chinese hosts grinned all the time we were there, and declared that "a true socialist does not believe in God."

Even though Christianity is tolerated, the school teachers often brush it all aside. There are said to be three million Christians in China. Catholicism is more frowned upon than Protestantism.

Most common of the old religions of China, and hardest to root out, is the belief in spirits which has been embraced by the great masses of poor peasants since ancient times. Families buried their dead themselves and then made sacrifices to their ghosts. This custom is now dying out, but not even the communist regime has dared to plough up the millions and millions of grave-mounds scattered all over the countryside.

Even though the communists refer to their own outlook on life as purely a political doctrine, it still bears many of the characteristics of a religion. There is a belief in a sort of paradise—that future happy state, where, in a struggle between good an evil, one must chose sides and where one can employ "the true faith" and solve all problems by reading his bible, Mao's "little red book." Many of the popular stories of what Mao meant are exceedingly close to the traditional miracle-legend. Chinese communism is also supported by a strong moral passion, which has caused many party officials to sacrifice their lives with the same implicit faith as any ancient Christian martyr. In the museum of the Revolution in Nanking, I have seen portraits of many communist heros, and relics in the form of diaries,

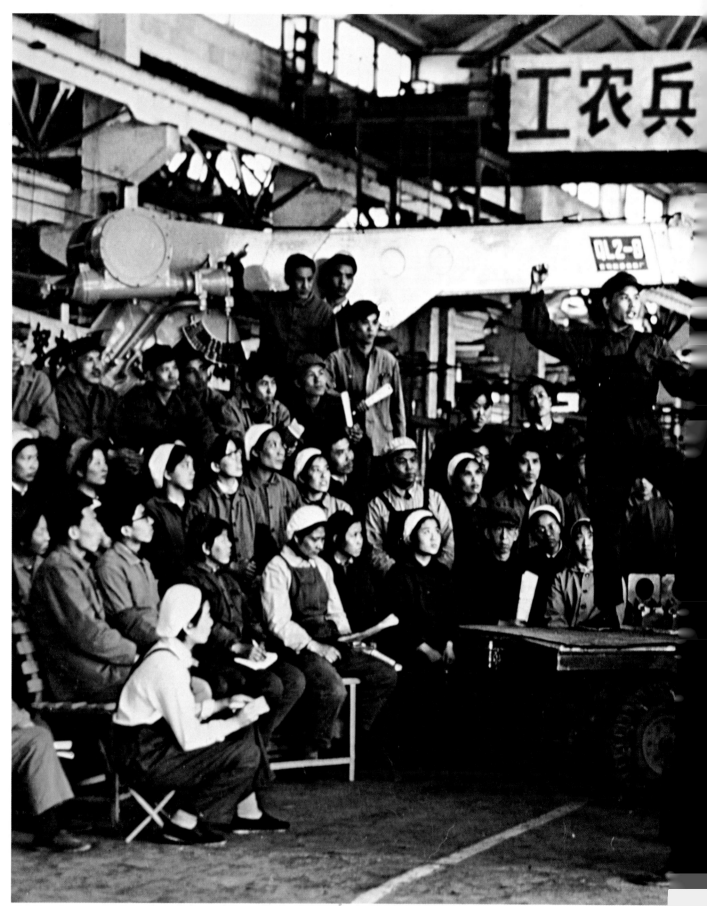

▲ *During and after the Cultural Revolution, Confucius, the deposed commander Lin Piao and others were regarded as class enemies. They were attacked in meetings in factories and in People's Communes.*

bloody shirts and the implements with which they were tortured. Every now and then, new diaries and stories are published about others—soldiers, nurses, truck drivers—who have died for the Revolution.

Many things suggest a comparison between the Cultural Revolution and the reformations which swept over religions in the past when they degenerated. It is no exaggeration to say that Mao Tse-tung was motivated toward his vision of a "just and classless society" and "the new man" by a zeal that was almost religious.

The dream of a new and better man exists in most religions. Christianity preaches that you must strive to be a good man even though you may find yourself in an evil society. The choice for a Christian therefore is between hypocrisy and despair and the goal of a moral life. Marx and the socialists preached that society will change when the economic system which is built on competition and exploitation has been abolished. The concept of "a new and better man" is as central to communism as it is to any other religion and without question, it applies in high degree to the communism of China.

An old lama priest midst the prayer-strips of his temple. We did not see any other believers. He was alone, and seemed to function like a dreamy and resigned museum caretaker. ▶

China experts like Anna Louise Strong and Han Suyin point out that the transformation of man is as important as economic and political reforms, and that it must happen simultaneously with them.

"It is well known that the final aim of China's Cultural Revolution is the making of a 'new man,' intelligently devoted not to self but to the community good."

"Transformation of man, transformation of his motivation and of the spiritual content of life, is just as necessary as the transformation of the Chinese earth." Han Suyin says in her book, *China in Year 2001*.

What could be more arresting to the stranger than meeting this "new man?" My own books and plays about China try to convey the underlying belief that in China we can see not only a new economic and political system, but people of an entirely new mold. The same thoughts occur to other visitors to China.

Recently I read an objective report by a group of American psychologists and sociologists who had been studying the nursery schools and education system in China. In the report one can sense a distrusting amazement and a reluctant enthusiasm. Such children as they found there just do not exist elsewhere —so cooperative and non-aggressive, so kind and selfless, so independent of sweets and toys and those thousand things which fill the lives of our children.

"The themes that had been developing in our observation of younger children continued through middle school. We were surprised at the extent to which Chinese adolescents—the word 'teenagers,' with its usual overtones, seems inappropriate—continued to be conforming, expressive, dutiful, well organized, and apparently devoted to the values expressed by adults," wrote the American, William Kessen, in his report *Childhood in China*.

What will this new man, this new ethic, mean to us, and what price will we be prepared to pay for it?

Every political system has its price—the Chinese do not deny that. Unlike some naive Maoists of the West, they have experienced the truth of Mao's pungent words:

"A revolution is not a dinner party. . . . A revolution is an insurrection, an act of violence by which one class overthrows another." The Chinese Revolution was a bloody business which took a toll of millions. It has been followed by a lot of "rectifying campaigns," that is, purging of class enemies, in which countless millions more have lost their lives. According to official information, during the campaign in 1952 alone, almost half of a million undesirable persons were executed. And still "the dictatorship of the proletariat" rules with limitations on freedom of speech and movement especially for the common people. In China, it is quickly seen how children and adults are exposed to an almost total ideological program. The only ideology allowed is communism. Within that framework there are heated debates, but no one dares to go outside the framework. During my visits to China I have never heard anyone say a single critical word against Mao.

A great part of the debate within the system has been conducted in the so-called "wall newspapers" (*bao dai*); that is, posters which are put up in working places and in educational institutions. In these *bao dai*, local party bosses are often criticized—even leaders as highly established as ministers—harshly and openly. The custom of wall newspapers was not invented by the cultural revolution. They are said to have existed in the fourteenth century A.D.

The Chinese themselves say that their tough discipline is as necessary as their military preparedness training. This is the price they pay to prevent famine and corruption, oppression and foreign domination. They feel that anyone who did not share their experiences in the time before the Revolution should refrain from passing criticism.

In view of this high price, it is amazing that so many young people from free democracies can find this strict state a temptation, an ideal, and a challenge. But, it is no wonder that starving underdeveloped countries do. Few countries, if any, have so quickly conquered such immense difficulties as has China. What fascinates all those Maoists in France, Germany, the Netherlands and in Sweden so? Is it because they believe they will find a purer and more consistent socialism in China than anywhere else in the world? Is it because they believe that Chinese communism is the remedy for the terrible injustices which still exist in the world? Or could it be because they feel the fulfillment of the eternal dream of a new and better man is at hand?

I have never been exposed to a more convulsive ideological upheaval than during my first two visits to China. One of the reasons may have been the void left by a lost religion. Values and views which I had believed to be unyielding were shaken: my faith in our democratic system, my distrust of militarism and moralism, my passion for the unlimited freedom of artists and authors. I cannot say that I have abandoned them all, but it was then that I saw for the first time how closely connected my values were to my situation as a privileged westerner and practitioner of a free profession. How would I choose if the right of a handful of authors to write what they wanted was to be weighed against the daily bread of millions of starving people?

Night after night I lay awake in hotel rooms with the sand from the Gobi Desert sticking to the sheets and wrestled with the same question over and over again: Is this what I have been looking for? Is this something for us, for my children? To escape the exploitation of one's fellow man, the dog-eat-dog mentality, criminality, prostitution, maladjusted youth, frustrated middle age and bitter old age—was it worth the Chinese price to escape all these?

Like a picture of Pearl Buck's China.

◀ *Will the Chinese be able to acomplish the eternal dream of a new and better man, and woman?*

Now, many years later, I have recovered from the shock and do not view the problem so dramatically. The Cultural Revolution, with its national exaggerations (for example, the ban on Beethoven's music), has confirmed what I have suspected for a long time: that the Chinese system as a whole cannot be exported. It is too dependent on the special background and mentality of the Chinese. We, with our traditions and our history, could never accept such a totalitarian ideology.

However, I still think that we have much to learn from the Chinese experiment with society and man:

> their attempt to produce a society without classes,
> their system of an annual period of manual work for everybody,
> their way of treating old people,
> their equality between the sexes, and
> their struggle to decentralize, and make the countryside as important as the towns.

And maybe most important of all:

> their conscious struggle to create other motives for social behavior than egoism, materialism or self-assertion.

Neither we nor the Chinese can produce a new man in the biological sense. But men and women with values other than material ones are not an unattainable goal.

For all of the book's 300 small scale pictures, Bo Gärtze used Canon SLR cameras.

CHINA
- The Dream of Man?

SOVIET UNION

Urumchi
◉

Sinkiang
☆

K a

T s i n g h a i

☆
Tibet

◉ *Lhasa*

S

NEPAL

BHUTAN

INDIA

PAKISTAN

BURMA

Kunm

Y ü n n

**BAY
OF BENGAL**

LA